ROADWAYS
to Success

Robert M. Sherfield
The Community College of Southern Nevada

James C. Williamson
Williamsburg Technical College

Debra A. McCandrew
Florence Darlington Technical College

ALLYN AND BACON

Boston · London · Toronto · Sydney · Tokyo · Singapore

Copyright © 1997 by Allyn and Bacon
A Viacom Company
160 Gould Street
Needham, MA 02194
www.abacon.com
America Online: keyword: College Online

All rights reserved. No part of the material protected by this copyright notice may be reproduced or utilized in any form or by any means, electronic or mechanical, including photocopying, recording, or by any information storage and retrieval system, without written permission from the copyright holder.

ISBN 0-205-18788-9

Senior vice president and Publisher: Nancy Forsyth
Series editorial assistant: Cheryl Ouellette
Executive marketing manager: Anne Harvey
Composition and prepress buyer: Linda Cox
Manufacturing buyer: Suzanne Lareau
Cover administrator: Linda Knowles
Cover designer: Susan Paradise
Photo researchers: Susan Duane and Martha Shethar
Production administrator: Susan Brown
Editorial-Production service: Colophon
Character illustrator: Drew Dernavich
Page layout: Christine Thompson

Printed in the United States of America
10 9 8 7 6 5 4 3 2 1   00 99 98 97 96

Photo Credits

Page 7 Brian Smith; page 9 Robert Harbison; page 18 Brian Smith; page 35 North Wind Picture Archives; page 36 Library of Congress; page 43 Chrysler Corporation; page 48 Richard Pasley/Stock Boston; page 62 Esbin-Anderson/The Image Works; page 63 Brian Smith; page 75 Robert Harbison; page 106 Anthony Neste; page 113 Adriana Rovers; page 117 Adriana Rovers; page 134 Robert Harbison; page 159 Brian Smith; page 193 Brian Smith; page 212 C. J. Allen/Stock Boston; page 228 Brian Smith; page 235 Brian Smith; page 249 (top) Robert Harbison, (bottom) Will Hart; page 253 Will Hart.

DEDICATION

Roadways to Success is dedicated to the many people who have helped us on our lifelong educational journeys. They paved the road, served as a beacon, and have gently altered our course through love, support, encouragement, and belief in us.

For Robb:
Brian Epps, MPIL
Neely Beaty
Beverly Jordan
Dick Smith

For Jimmie:
Kim and Jordan Williamson
Jake, Louise, David, and Nancy Williamson
Robert and Betty Dickens
Miss Ethel Williamson
Mr. Ervin Faulkenberry
Dr. Glenn Thomas
Dr. June Mohler
Dr. Mary T. Littlejohn

For Debi:
James and Alyce McCandrew
Chuck and Bobbi Montanye

PROFESSIONAL ACKNOWLEDGMENTS

A number of very talented reviewers helped us develop and hone this book. Many thanks go to: Stan Coberly, West Virginia University at Parkersburg; Carol Cohen, Edgewood College; John Lanning, University of Colorado, Denver; Judy Lynch, Kansas State University; and Darlene Pabis, Westmoreland County Community College.

We are also grateful for the support from:
Dr. Richard Moore, President, Community College of Southern Nevada; Dr. Robert M. Silverman, Senior Vice-President Academic Affairs, CCSN; Dr. Don Smith, Department Chair, English, CCSN; Dr. Norman Scott, President, Williamsburg Technical College; Dr. Larry Cline, Vice-President for Academic and Student Affairs, CCTC; Anna Strange, Dean of Arts and Sciences, CCTC; Dr. Rose Johnson, Vice President for Corporate and Continuing Education, Forsyth Technical Community College; Dr. Charles Gould, President, Florence Darlington Technical College; Dr. Charles Muse, Vice President for Academic Affairs, FDTC; Dr. Sandra Griffin, Dean of Learning Resource Center, FDTC; Gail Figa, Department Chair, Transitional Studies, FDTC

Jane Lucas
George L. Bistany, Jr.
Hattie Pinckney
Betty Boatwright
Lynne Bratton
Kate Wagstaffe

and
Nancy Forsyth

CONTENTS

TO THE STUDENT ix
ABOUT THE AUTHORS xi

1 FINE-TUNING YOUR VEHICLE
Recognizing Your Potential and Building Self-Esteem 1

Why Are You Here? 6
Where Are You Going? 8
Discovering and Achieving Your Potential 12
Personal Values 15
The Values Auction 15
Self-Esteem 17
What Is Self-Esteem? 18
Why Is Self-Esteem Important? 18
Developing Positive Self-Esteem 18
■ Roadways to Increasing Your Self-Esteem 23
Observations: Charting Your Course, Looking Beyond, Your Next Step 28

2 MAPPING YOUR JOURNEY
Goal Setting and Motivation 31

What Do These People Have in Common? 35
Eliminating Fear 36
What Is a Goal? 41
Why Are Goals Important? 42
Types of Goals 43
How to Write a Goal 44
What Is an Objective? 45
Roadblocks to Success: Barriers to Achieving Your Goals 46
Traveling the Road on Your Own: Motivation 48
What Is Motivation? 49
Why Is Motivation Important? 49

■ Roadways to Reaching Your Goals 52
Goal-Setting Worksheet 53
Write A Short-Term Goal 54
Write A Long-Term Goal 54
Observations 55

3 PLANNING TO REACH YOUR DESTINATION ON TIME
Time Management 57

Time Analysis 60
Facts about Time 62
Different Types of Time 62
Understanding How Time Passes 64
Putting Real Time to Work 65
Where Does Your Time Go? 66
Your Study Time 69
Your Study Plan 72
Leading Time Wasters 73
Procrastination: The Enemy of the Student 74
It Is All about Priorities! 75
Remember!! 76
■ Roadways to Effective Time Management 77
Time-Management Tips 77
Observations 77

4 SIGHTS, SOUNDS AND SENSATIONS
Information Processing and Learning Styles 79

Information-Processing Theory 83
Characteristics of Analytical and Global Thinkers 86
Analytical Processing or Thinking 88
Global Processing or Thinking 88
Brain Teaser 88
Learning Preference Theory 89

How Do You Learn? 91
   Visual Learners 93
   Auditory Learners 94
   Kinesthetic Learners 94
Using Mnemonic Devices 95
■ **Roadways to Learning and Processing Information** 97
Observations 98

5 SCANNING THE RADIO
The Powerful Art of Listening 101

To Be a Captain, You First Have to Be a Sailor 105
The Difference between Listening and Hearing 106
Practical Definitions of Listening 110
Obstacles to Listening 113
   Obstacle One: Prejudging 113
   Obstacle Two: Talking 114
   Obstacle Three: Bringing Your Emotions to the Table 115
   Active and Passive Listening Characteristics 116
How Do I Get Others to Listen to Me? 117
Listening for Key Words, Phrases, and Hints 118
   The Top Ten Reasons for Actively Listening 119
Test Your Listening Skills 120
■ **Roadways to Active Listening** 126
Observations 127

6 CHARTING YOUR JOURNEY
The Process of Note Taking 129

Why Take Notes? 133
Do I Need to Write That Down? 134
Preparing to Take Notes 135
Roadways of Effective Note Taking 135
   Attend Class 135
   Come to Class Prepared 136
   Bring Your Text to Class 136
   Ask Questions and Participate in Class!!! 137
   Now We're Ready to Begin the Learning Process 137
The L-STAR System 137
   L—Listening 138
   S—Setting It Down 138
   T—Translating 140
   A—Analyzing 140
   R—Remembering 141
Putting It All Together: Note-Taking Techniques 141
   The Outline Technique 142

The Cornell (Modified Cornell, Split-Page or T) System 143
The Mapping System 145
■ **Roadways to Effective Note Taking** 151
Observations 151

7 DRIVER TRAINING
Learning How to Study 153

Homework? Studying? Who Needs It? 156
Attending Class 157
Getting Organized 158
What Notebook Systems Do You Use? 158
When Do You Study? 158
Where Do You Study? 159
Study Supplies 160
A Study Plan 161
Roadways of Studying 162
Learning Vocabulary 162
   Context Clues 163
   Word Analysis 164
Reading and Using Textbooks 165
The SQ3R Method 167
   Step 1: Survey 168
   Step 2: Question 168
   Step 3: Read 168
   Step 4: Recite 168
   Step 5: Review 169
Highlighting Your Textbook 169
Practicing the SQ3R 170
Reviewing Class and Textbook Notes 176
Studying Math 177
■ **Roadways to Studying Effectively** 179
Observations 180

8 OBTAINING YOUR LICENSE
Test-Taking Strategies 183

Why Do I Have to Take a Test? 188
Controlling Test Anxiety 188
■ **Roadways to Reducing Text Anxiety** 190
Preparing for Tests 190
   The Dreamer 191
   The Procrastinator 191
   The Planner 191

- Roadways to Preparing for a Test 192
    - Test-Taking Strategies 192
    - General Test-Taking Techniques 193
    - Strategies for Answering Matching Questions 194
    - Strategies for Answering True/False Questions 195
    - Strategies for Answering Multiple-Choice Questions 195
    - Strategies for Answering Short-Answer Questions 197
    - Strategies for Answering Essay Questions 197
    - Observations 199

9 STOPPING TO ASK FOR DIRECTIONS
Campus Resources 201

- The Importance of Resources 204
- Tangible Versus Intangible Resources 205
- The Owner's Manual: Your College Catalog 206
- The Library 209
- Computer Resources: A Trip Along the Information Superhighway 210
- Making a Pit Stop: Learning Resource Centers 211
- Traveling Companions: Your Friends 212
- Counseling Services 213
- Financial Aid Services 213
    - Student Eligibility for Federal Financial Aid 214
- Roadways for Applying for Financial Aid 216
    - Health Services 217
    - The Next Step 218
    - Observations 219

10 ENJOYING THE JOURNEY
Understanding the Professorate 221

- High School Teachers Versus College Professors: What's the Difference? 225
- Why We Teach in a College 227
- The Life of a Professor 227
- Academic Freedom and What It Means to You 229
- Understanding What the Professor Wants 231
- What Makes a Good Student 232
- What Makes a Good Professor 233
- Classroom Etiquette 234
- Reading the Professor's Schedule 236
- Observations 238

11 REACHING YOUR DESTINATION
Career Planning 241

- What Do You Want to Be When You Grow Up? 245
- Daydreaming 247
- Do You Want to Do Something or Be Something? 248
- Help Me! I'm Undeclared! 250
- Seven Steps to Career Decision Making 250
    - Step One: Dream! 250
    - Step Two: Talk to Your Advisor 251
    - Step Three: Using College Electives 251
    - Step Four: Go to the Career Center 251
    - Step Five: Read! Read! Read! 252
    - Step Six: Shadowing 252
    - Step Seven: Joining Preprofessional Organizations 252
- What Is a Mentor? 253
- What Is a Career Counselor? 255
- Once You Know Where You Are Going, How Do You Get There? 256
- Will I Work with People, Things, or Ideas? 256
- How Much Training Am I Going to Need to Do this Job? 257
- How Much Money Will I Make in this Profession? 257
- Do I Know Anyone Who Already Works in this Profession? 257
- Will I Work Indoors or Outdoors? 258
- Will the Work I Do Be Mental or Physical? 258
- Where Will I Live While Doing this Job? 258
- Will I Travel with this Job? 259
- Would I Want to Do this for the Rest of My Life? 259
- Develop a Personal Success Plan 259
- Observations 260
- My Career Research Plan 261

REFERENCES 264

GLOSSARY 265

INDEX 273

TO THE STUDENT

Today is going to be the very best day of your life. You may not have known that when you got out of bed this morning, but if you so choose, today is going to be one of the most important, one of the most significant, and one of the most challenging days of your life. Today, just like every day, you will have the opportunity to begin again—you get to start over. How wonderful!

For some of you, your thousand-mile journey will begin today. For others, today will be the day that you find a new road, a new path, or a new light. Still, for others, today will be just another day—standing still. The choice is yours. That's what this book is all about—making informed choices, making choices that may affect the rest of your life.

This textbook, *Roadways to Success*, is intended to show you how to begin anew. It is written to give you the power to choose any path, any road, or any highway. This book, if used as your instructor guides you, will take you on a self-discovery journey that will give you the tools to help you raise your self-esteem, become a more effective student, develop personal responsibility, and hopefully, lead you toward a brighter future.

This is your book. Use it! Write in it, mark in it, use highlighters, dogear the pages, write notes to yourself in it. The only way that this book cannot help you is if you leave it at home or never read it.

There are several common elements within this book that are included to assist you on your journey. Each chapter begins with a story about an actual student who has struggled with and overcome many of the obstacles that you might face in the days and months ahead. Each chapter also includes a segment called, "Self-Study." It is included to help you assess where you stand in relation to the content to be covered in the chapter. Each chapter also has a variety of activities and questions that, when answered with thought and consideration, will help you become a more successful student. At the end of each chapter is a activity called "As a Result of this Chapter . . . ." This will help you keep a log of the most important things you have learned from this course.

Remember, the journey begins today. Make sure that you have your bags packed and your goals aimed high. The sky is the limit!

The journey of a thousand miles, begins with a single step.

Chinese proverb

ABOUT THE AUTHORS

Robert M. Sherfield

Robert Sherfield has been teaching public speaking, theater, and study skills and working with first-year orientation programs for over 13 years. Currently, he is on the full-time faculty at the Community College of Southern Nevada, teaching both study skills and orientation courses and is Director of Tutorial Services and Learning Resources.

Robb's extensive work with student success programs includes experience with the design and implementation of these programs—including one program that was presented at the International Conference on the Freshman Year Experience in Newcastle upon Tyne, England.

Some of Robb's responsibilities have also included serving as Coordinator of University 101, Director of Student and Cultural Activities, Director of Orientation Programs, and Director of Student Media at the University of South Carolina at Union. He also codesigned a student success course at Florence Darlington Technical College.

In addition to his coauthorship of *Roadways to Success*, he has also coauthored *Cornerstone: Building on Your Best* (Allyn & Bacon, 1997) and the trade book, *365 Things I Learned in College* (Allyn & Bacon, 1996).

Robb's interest in student success began with his own first year in college. Low SAT scores and a mediocre high school ranking denied him entrance into college. With the help of a success program, Robb was granted entrance into college, and went on to earn a doctorate and become a college faculty member. He has always been interested in the social, academic, and cultural development of students, and sees this book as his way to contribute to the positive development of first-year students across the nation.

James C. Williamson

Jimmie Williamson currently serves as Dean of Instruction at Williamsburg Technical College, located in South Carolina. With over 15 years of post-secondary work, Jimmie has served as either a faculty member or an administrator in public, private, two- and four-year institutions. Having served as a Dean of Student Affairs and a Registrar, Jimmie is very familiar with the struggles and frustrations faced by under-prepared college students.

Jimmie co-designed a student success course at Florence Darlington Technical College. He was twice honored at the University of South Carolina at Union as a "Teacher of the Year Nominee," which was a direct result of his work with the University 101 Program. Jimmie has presented at the National Conference on the Freshman Year Experience as well as at the Adult Learner Conference.

Because of his own struggle with selecting a college major, Jimmie has become extremely interested in the career selection process. As a result, he has used his counseling background to assist other first-year students (and students in transition) in making career decisions. It is his hope that this book will provide the student with the tools and information necessary to make educated and informed career choices.

Debra A. McCandrew

Debi currently serves as a developmental math and study skills instructor at Florence Darlington Technical College, located in South Carolina. Having worked in education for 11 years, Debi has taught at the secondary and post-secondary level and has worked as an assistant director in a hospital-based learning disabilities center.

Debi's early work in study skills began when she was hired to write the script for a study skills video. Extensive research in study strategies provided the skills to complete the video, an instructor's manual, and numerous community-based study skills programs. "Training the Trainer" has enabled Debi to work in both public and private sectors of secondary and post-secondary education.

Debi was a presenter at the National "At Risk Conference" and has conducted numerous in-services including a learning styles presentation for the South Carolina State Department of Education. Her significant work in learning styles, study techniques, and a commonsense approach to academic work enhances her contribution to the book. Debi believes that every student, regardless of where they begin, can achieve academic excellence; this belief continues to motivate her to work with under-prepared, first-year students.

CHAPTER 1

Fine Tuning Your Vehicle
Recognizing Your Potential and Building Self-Esteem

CHAPTER 1

Life is about change and about movement and about becoming something other than what you are at this very moment.

Unknown

◆ I remember walking to the mailbox and getting the letter from my "college of choice." As I walked back toward the house, every dream I had of a college education passed before my eyes. "We regret to inform you that because of your SAT scores and your high school rank, your application has been denied."

I was not the best student in the world. Looking back, I was not even average. I passed senior English with the grade of D minus. My predicted grade point average (GPA) for college was a mere 0.07. I never knew how to study. I never asked for any assistance. I did not even know how to properly use the library. I now faced having to continue working in the textile plant instead of going to college.

Two days later, another letter came to me from the college. It was signed by the director of the Summer Prep Program. They offered me a second chance. Their letter stated that if I would come to the summer session and make at least a B average, I would be admitted as a temporary student. The weight of the world was on my shoulders. How could I, a D- high school student, take four classes in *college* and score a B? Quickly, and I mean very quickly, I learned how to ask for help. I went to the Assistance Lab and the first thing I learned was *how* to study. I studied and I studied and I studied. At the end of four weeks, I had three A's and a B. I had made it!

Those 4 weeks were the easy part. I had changed and I knew that I could never go back. I had a taste for something that could only be quenched in college—a taste for knowledge. My name is Robert Sherfield and eighteen years later as I co-author your text, I find myself *teaching* college. This was possible because I assumed responsibility for my future and I learned how to study.

This book is intended to be a guide to show *you* how to assume responsibility for your own learning, which will enable you to make the most of your education and your future. It is our hope to show you that learning can be one of the most rewarding and exciting experiences of your life. Right now, you may or may not see it that way. You may have had some experiences that were not positive or you may be in college because your parents or someone insisted that you enroll. Your interests may be in getting a quick degree or re-training for a promotion at work. That's OK. The primary concern at this moment is developing the basic skills that will allow you to graduate and move into the world of work, get that promotion, or move on to a four-year degree.

How do you feel about being enrolled in this course? You may be upset at this moment because you were required to take this course or because you were required to enroll in a developmental studies program. Many freshman feel the same way. They do not want to "waste" their time in classes that may carry only one hour of credit or carry no degree credit. It may be that this course does not count toward your graduation credit hours. At some schools, however, it does.

One day, a professor heard a group of students complaining about having to take developmental courses. When she came around the corner of the hallway, they froze with fear, knowing that she had heard them talking. They were right, she had heard them. She stopped to ask how they were doing, sat on the bench with them, and told them something that made a huge difference in their lives. "I know that you are upset for having to enroll in classes that won't transfer or count toward graduation," she said, "but without these classes, there will be no graduation for you. This program is not a punishment, but a second chance for you. So many people never get a second chance, but this school cares about you. You can look at it as punishment or you can look at it as the first day of the rest of your life. *You* have to make that decision."

Most of the group chose to take her words seriously because they knew in their hearts that they lacked the skills to make it to graduation. As college *graduates*, most students who enrolled in developmental studies courses can tell you, without hesitation, that study skills and orientation courses work. Research case after research case proves how freshmen who enroll in orientation or study skills courses graduate in higher numbers than those who do not take them (Gardner & Jeweler, 1995). This course gives you another chance. It makes today the first day of the rest of your life.

Your college cares about you and your success, or this course would not exist. The faculty and administration of your college have devoted countless hours to developing and designing a course that will help you to become the very best that you can be. They believe in you, and they want to provide you with the tools to allow you to believe in yourself. This is their life's work. It is now your responsibility to assume responsibility for your education through the services being offered at your college.

If you complete the exercises in this chapter, participate in class, read the additional assignments that may be issued by your professor, and keep an open mind, at the end of this chapter, you will be able to

- Determine why you are in college
- Evaluate your past educational experiences
- Define success and identify successful people in your life
- Use your inner potential
- Evaluate your value system
- Complete a personal analysis of yourself
- Define self-esteem and describe why it is important
- Use Roadways to Increasing Self-Esteem

The following ten questions are intended to cause you to think about your potential and self-esteem at this point in your life. Take a moment and answer each statement carefully.

SELF-STUDY

1. I am serious about my future.   *1 2 3 4 5*
2. I study at least two hours per night per course.
   1 2 3 4 5
3. I enjoy school.
   1 2 3 4 5
4. Learning is fun to me.
   1 2 3 4 5
5. I take risks. *1 2 3 4 5*

6. I expect a great deal from myself.   *1 2 3 4 5*
7. I often think about my future.   *1 2 3 4 5*
8. I plan for my success.
   1 2 3 4 5
9. I have high self-esteem.
   1 2 3 4 5
10. I am a positive person.
    1 2 3 4 5

5=Strongly Agree
4=Agree
3=Don't Know
2=Disagree
1=Strongly Disagree

TOTAL YOUR POINTS from the ten questions above. Refer to the rating scale below to determine where you stand in relation to your potential and self-esteem development.

0–10   *You do not think a great deal about your future or your potential. You devote little time to planning and working toward success.*

11–20   *You give some thought to success and your potential, but you do not spend a great deal of time seriously considering your future.*

21–30   *You spend an average amount of time thinking about your future and planning for success.*

31–40   *You devote more than an average amount of time to planning and developing your potential. You think about success often and have probably developed a plan for success.*

41–50   *You think about your future and your potential. You have learned to put into place the strategies for achieving success and high self-esteem.*

How did you do? Does your score represent what you know about yourself? If your score is not positive to you right now, relax. This chapter and the following chapters in this book will give you the skills to help you develop your potential and realize your goals.

Why Are You Here?

It does not matter if you are starting college, or if you are in your second semester, or if you are a sophomore, you have probably asked yourself from time to time, "How did I get here?" or "Why am I really sitting in this class?" What answers come to your mind? Your first thoughts might have been

1. I want to be a better person.

2. My parents made me come.

3. I have nowhere else to be.

4. My friends came, so I did too.

5. Job re-training.

6. Personal or professional crisis.

7. To provide a better life for my family.

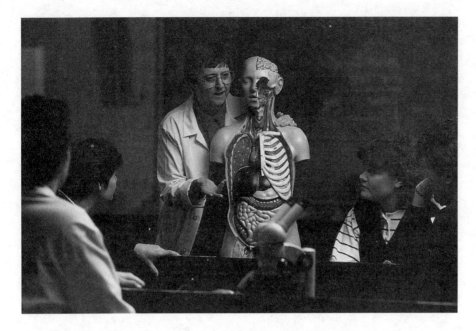

The first key to success in most endeavors is deciding to take action. You've done that by enrolling in college. Secondly, you probably have a good idea why you are here and what you want to accomplish.

Using the spaces below, list the reasons why you have chosen to attend college:

1. _____
2. _____
3. _____
4. _____

Was it hard to come up with your list, or did you jot down your thoughts quickly? Why? If it was difficult, perhaps it is because most of us spend so little time actually thinking about our education and what it really means to our future. The next few questions are intended to get you thinking about college on a different level. Take your time responding to each question.

Is learning an enjoyable experience? _____

Why or why not? _____

_____

_____

_____

How could learning become a more enjoyable experience for you? _____

_____

_____

_____

RECOGNIZING YOUR POTENTIAL AND BUILDING SELF-ESTEEM

What are the major ideas you must consider in making learning and school a more enjoyable experience? Below, list what you feel your school could do to make learning more enjoyable for you.

1. _____
2. _____
3. _____
4. _____

List what you feel your teachers could do to make learning more enjoyable for you.

1. _____
2. _____
3. _____
4. _____

Most importantly, list the ways that you can bring about change. How can you make learning and school a more enjoyable experience?

1. _____
2. _____
3. _____
4. _____

    A great part of your success in college is realizing that *you* can bring about change. You've just begun by spending time evaluating your current situation. Remember, it is hard to play ball when you're not on the field.

Where Are You Going?

    Robert Frost, a famous poet, wrote a poem about two roads splitting in a forest and his decision to take "the one less traveled." Today, you are faced with the same decision. There are two roads for you. One will be filled with challenges and hard work. The other will be the road that, unfortunately, many students take: the road that avoids challenge, that sidesteps opportunity, and

> *I have learned that success is to be measured not so much by the position one has reached in life, as by the obstacles which they have overcome while trying to succeed.*
>
> **Booker T. Washington, American educator**

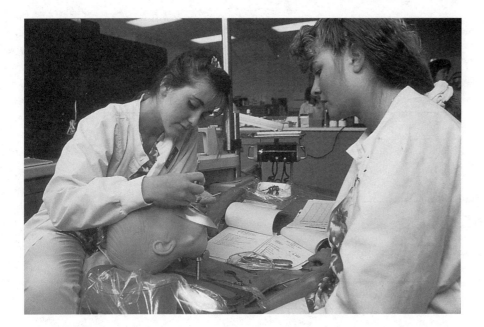

the road that often leads to dropping out of college. Which road will you take? Only you can make that decision, and it will not be an easy one. Whatever your ultimate goal might be, it will be important for you to map out a course to get there and then learn to take the proper roadways. Success does not happen without a plan. In the coming days, you will begin to realize that your road will look differently, ride differently, and feel differently from that of your friends. Everyone's path to success is different, and only you can map your course.

The following questions are intended to help you begin to develop a philosophy about success and what you can do to bring about success in your life.

Below, write your definition of success:

_____
_____
_____
_____

Describe one person in your life whom you consider to be successful. Why are they successful? _____
_____
_____

Below, list the one accomplishment you want to achieve more than anything else:

_____
_____
_____

RECOGNIZING YOUR POTENTIAL AND BUILDING SELF-ESTEEM

Why? _____
_____
_____
_____
_____

Now, how do you plan to achieve this? _____
_____
_____
_____
_____
_____

What part does your education play in reaching this goal? _____
_____
_____
_____
_____
_____

What do you need to do to make sure this goal is reached? _____
_____
_____
_____
_____
_____

What part does this course play in reaching your goal? _____
_____
_____
_____
_____
_____

One of the most important lessons to be learned about beginning a journey is that the road will sometimes change. Have you ever been driving to a friend's house and you decided to do a couple of unexpected things along the way, like stop at the store, pick up another friend, or take a different road? The road to your friend's house changed, didn't it? Keep in mind that when beginning your journey to success, your road will most likely change several times. There is no harm in changing your mind. The harm lies in traveling down a road that no longer suits you and your ideas.

A DEFINITION OF SUCCESS

"To laugh often and much; to win the respect of intelligent people and the affection of children; to earn the appreciation of honest critics and endure the betrayal of false friends; to appreciate beauty; to find the best in others; to leave the world a bit better, whether by a healthy child, a garden patch, or a redeemed social condition; to know even one life has breathed easier because you have lived. This is to have Succeeded!"

Unknown

There are probably as many definitions of success as there are people in the world. The poem defining success gives us a look at how many ways we can succeed. Thinking positively and realizing that one failure or one setback does *not* make us failures or unsuccessful people is a step toward success. It only means that we have to try harder and concentrate on the many positive aspects of our lives. Our setbacks can help us see our potential.

There is a joke about a man who was asked if he could play the violin and he answered, "I don't know. I've never tried." Those who have never tried to play a violin really do not know whether they can or not. Those who say too early in life and too firmly, "No, I'm not at all musical," shut themselves off from whole areas of life that might have proved rewarding. In each of us, there are unknown possibilities, undiscovered potentialities—and one big advantage of having an open self-concept rather than a rigid one is that we shall continue to expose ourselves to new experiences and therefore, we shall continue to discover more and more about ourselves as we grow older.

Adler

Discovering and Achieving Your Potential

Ironically, one of the things we know least about ourselves is what we are capable of and how great our potential can be. It has been said that we use only 1% of our brain capacity. It has further been suggested that of the 400,000-plus words in the English language, the average educated person uses only 2,000 of them. Discovering your potential is an ongoing process that hopefully lasts for a lifetime.

You are always discovering new things you can do and new ideas that can help you live a productive life. When was the last time that you did something you thought couldn't be done? One of the keys to a successful life is analyzing your potential and setting your goals. Many times, students let other people determine what they will be able to do for the rest of their lives. For some of you, because of poor math performance, you may never choose to be an architect or physicist. Math may simply not be your strongest area. This does not mean that you can't do math, it simply means that you may have to try harder in this subject area. Others may find that in the areas of art, music, theater, English, literature, hobbies, crafts, and people skills, their possibilities are limitless. It does not mean that they will use these skills as their life's work. You have to look beyond what you are capable of at this very moment to discover your true potential. In other words, don't cut yourself short just because problems may arise in certain areas.

The first step to discovering your potential is deciding what you value the most in your life. Is it playing the violin, becoming a physical therapist, or repairing a car? Do you enjoy working with people, with numbers, indoors or outdoors? All of these endeavors are worthy; you will be the one to make the final decision regarding your actions. To add even more confusion to the situation, you are going to meet people who have interests very different from your own, and they may introduce you to other areas of interests. This can be helpful and confusing at the same time, but if you allow yourself to think and experience these differences with an open mind, you will begin to grow in ways you never imagined possible. You will have given yourself a broader base from which to build. Who ever said that you could do only one thing? You need to decide where your interests lie and how those interests could best be expanded and enjoyed throughout your life and career. Experiencing new challenges and meeting new people will help you discover and evaluate your greatest potential.

The next exercise will assist you in beginning an evaluation of your life and your potential. Some of these questions are going to be a bit difficult because you may have never thought about them and you probably have never written down the answers before. Take as much time as you need to answer these questions truthfully and completely.

List three things you expect of yourself:

1. _____
2. _____
3. _____

List five things you consider yourself to be capable of, interested in, and/or talented in:

1. _____
2. _____
3. _____
4. _____
5. _____

Now, list why you consider yourself to be capable, interested, or talented in these things:

1. _____
2. _____
3. _____
4. _____
5. _____

List five things that interest you but that you consider yourself to be less capable or talented in:

1. _____
2. _____
3. _____
4. _____
5. _____

List why you believe that you are less capable or talented in these areas:

1. _____

2. _____
3. _____
4. _____
5. _____

More than likely, you listed reasons such as "I do not spend enough time on it," " I am not as committed as I should be," " I am afraid of what people will say," and so forth. Many times our potential is limited by our lack of practice, time, commitment, or our fear that we may be thought of as different.

When a friend was in elementary school, he took piano lessons and all of the guys found out. It was not easy for him to continue, and eventually, the teasing and name calling led him to quit. He said that many times he regretted the decision to quit. There had always been something inside of him that cried out every time he passed a piano. He said, "I always have to sit down and play." Apparently, his potential in that area had never been realized. He recently said that he bought a piano and discovered that he had talent. He said, "I may never be a famous pianist like Chopin or Beethoven, but that piano has brought me a great deal of pleasure and challenge." Realizing our potential *requires* us to conduct an evaluation of ourselves, our interests, our values, and our dreams. It requires us to take risks. So often in this life, we let others tell us what to do and we let them choose our future. It is only when we go through a self-analysis that we set our goals and begin our journey toward achieving our true potential. Always remember:

$${SE} + P \times M = S$$

Self-Esteem + Potential x Motivation = Success

Simply stated, this means that when we are sure of ourselves and like ourselves, and if we realize our potential and find the motivation to make our dreams come true, success will most likely follow.

Personal Values

What do you value most in your life? A great part of discovering our potential means evaluating questions that help us see more clearly where we are going—and from where we have come. So many times, we concern ourselves with our friends, our family, or someone else, but spend very little time thinking about our own lives. Has this happened to you? This section of the book is designed to allow you to spend some time with yourself, your values, your ideas, and your life.

In the next section, you will be given an imaginary $100. You may spend the money any way that you choose based on your value system. Contrast how your values differ from those around you. Your professor will assist you with this exercise.

The Values Auction

Directions: There are ten items listed. You can bid in $5 increments. It may be that you want to bid $5 on each item, $10 on ten items or $100 on one item. You can not spend over $100 in total. If someone out–bids you, you can move money from any item that you have not purchased. Example: If you have a written bid of $35 on "A satisfying religion" and someone bids $40, you can move money from any item to out–bid that person as long as you do not spend over $100. Be sure to record the top bid for which the item sold so that you can compare how your views and values may differ from that of your classmates.

THE AUCTION

Item To Be Bought	My Budget	Top Bid
A happy marriage and family	$_____	$_____
A chance to be president	$_____	$_____

The love of friends	$_____	$_____
Self-esteem and confidence	$_____	$_____
A healthy life	$_____	$_____
A world free of prejudice	$_____	$_____
To understand the meaning of life	$_____	$_____
Success in a chosen profession	$_____	$_____
A satisfying religion	$_____	$_____
Unlimited power	$_____	$_____

After the auction is over, your professor will ask you why you bid money on a certain item. Listen carefully to your peers and compare their reasons for bidding on an item or not bidding on an item to your own reasons. You'll be surprised how different, and how alike you may be.

What is the item for which you bid the most money? _____

Why? _____

_____

_____

_____

_____

For which item did you bid the least amount of money? _____

Why? _____

_____

_____

_____

_____

Value systems differ greatly, and it is only when we understand our own values that we can truly begin to appreciate the values of others. This is somewhat complicated by the fact that building self-esteem means knowing ourselves and our values, but it is almost impossible to know what we value without a positive self-esteem. We have to work on both issues at the same time and treat both with care and detail.

Self-Esteem

Another area that you will need to consider on the road to achieving your full potential is your self-esteem. Just as you are the only one who can identify and realize your own potential, you are the only one who can give yourself worth. You can be told a thousand times a day that you are kind, gentle, caring, giving, smart, handsome, pretty, or talented, but until you believe in your own strengths, kindness, intellect, looks, or talents, you can never have high self-esteem. The way you feel about yourself determines how you treat other people. Only the very strong people in this world can be sensitive and caring. It is the weak and those with low a self-esteem who are cruel and insensitive. Re-read that statement and consider it carefully. Often we think of this situation in the other direction, don't we? However, it is only the people who love and respect themselves who can love and respect others. When you begin to discover your potential, you begin to build your self-esteem.

A person who doubts himself is like a man who would enlist in the ranks of his enemies and bear arms against himself. He makes his failure certain by himself being the first person to be convinced of it.

W. Purkey, educator

What Is Self-Esteem?

Much research has been done in the areas of self-esteem and self-worth. Basically, self-esteem is the picture or photograph that you hold of yourself in your own mind. It is the value you place on who you are and what you are worth. Your self-esteem is learned; you are not born with a self-esteem. You develop your self-esteem by the people you are around from birth. The most important aspect of self-esteem is that no one can give it to you, but many people may try to lower it.

Why Is Self-Esteem Important?

Low self-esteem has been linked to many problems in our society. The lack of self-esteem has been traced to poor performance in school, crime, homelessness, teen pregnancy, and even AIDS, to name a few social and academic problems. William Purky, a psychologist, found that there was a direct relationship between self-esteem and academic achievement. Purky also found a relationship between self-esteem and how much people contribute to society. He said, "People with higher self-esteem are more aware of the needs not only of themselves, but of society as a whole. They tend to be more productive members of society and contribute more to the good of the whole population."

Developing Positive Self-Esteem

If you have low self-esteem, you are not going to be able to increase your self-esteem overnight; however, there are ways to begin to develop self-esteem that may have some immediate

Building self-esteem comes with reclaiming that part of ourselves that we put on the sidelines because we felt we didn't deserve to be happy.

Robinson

impact. Building positive self-esteem is a process that takes time. The process should be taken in steps. This section of the chapter is designed to assist you in recognizing some important facts about yourself and assist you in building a higher self-esteem. Spend some time with these questions and answer them truthfully.

What is the most important statement that you can make about your life?

_____
_____
_____

List five things that you like most about yourself.

1. _____

Why? _____
_____

2. _____

Why? _____
_____

3. _____

Why? _____
_____

4. _____

Why? _____
_____

5. _____
Why? _____
_____

Now, list the five things that you would like to improve on or change about yourself and tell why.

1. _____

Why? _____
_____

2. _____

Why? _____
_____

3. _____

Why? _____
_____

4. _____

Why? _____
_____

5. _____

Why? _____
_____

Do you consider yourself to be a positive or negative person? _____

Why? _____
_____
_____

How do you think others see you? _____
_____
_____
_____

In this space below, write an advertisement about yourself. _____
_____
_____
_____
_____

How do you really view yourself? What is the picture you hold in your mind of your life? Many times, you tend to see the bad more clearly then the good, don't you? If you study your responses above, you will find that you probably spend much of your time concentrating on the things you like least about yourself, and not nearly enough time concentrating on the things that are beautiful and positive in your life.

Building positive self-esteem is mathematical. It simply requires you to subtract and add. It requires you to subtract or take away those things in your life that are negative or the things that cause you to feel bad. It may mean that you have to subtract people, jobs, or even objects from your life. However, building a more positive self-esteem also means that you have to do some addition in your life as well. You have to add things to your life that make you feel good and positive. You can add friends, a new job, a college education, or a new environment.

List three things that make you feel good in your life:

1. _____
2. _____
3. _____

List three things that make you feel bad in your life:

1. _____
2. _____
3. _____

Study the list above. What have you done in the past week to eliminate the bad or negative aspects of your life? _____

_____

_____

From the list above, what have you done to make sure that you have added the positive aspects to your life in the past week? _____

_____

_____

As mentioned earlier, a child is not born with a self-esteem. Children learn their worth from their caregivers. Often, you learn what you can or cannot do through your association with other people, not yourself. Many times, you may be told, "You'll never be able to do that" or "You're not smart enough to do that." You've heard the old expression, "Tell a child he is dumb long enough, and he'll believe it." All too often, you begin to believe what others tell you about yourself and fail to listen to your inner voice that says, *"Yes,* I can."

When was the last time your negative thoughts came true? _____

_____

_____

Why were your thoughts negative on the issue? _____

_____

_____

Do you believe that others' actions or words led you to fail? _____

_____

After studying the answers to the questions above, you can now see how negative thoughts from others, from yourself, or your inner voice can cause your self-esteem to be lowered. You now must look at ways to build a more positive self-esteem.

It has been said that the only way to conquer fear is to face it head on. The same is true with building self-esteem. The only way to build a positive self-esteem is to note your short-comings and do your best to correct them. The best way to correct short-comings is to take them one at a time. For example, if you listed a fear of public speaking or a lack of public speaking skills as one of the things you would like to improve about yourself, you would want to develop a plan that would allow you to correct the situation slowly. You would need to map out a course that would raise your self-esteem in the area of public speaking. For example:

- Choose one person in class whom you do not know very well and begin a conversation with that person.

- Accept an invitation to a party where you know only a few people. You will then be forced to talk with others.

- The next time you have an oral report due in history, biology, or English, look at it as an opportunity, not as a tragedy.

- If you are asked to speak at church or a club meeting, accept the challenge, no matter how difficult it may seem.

- Take a public speaking course as an elective.

This type of planning and risk taking could ease your fear of speaking in public and raise your self-esteem as well. It may not happen overnight. It may take months or years, but at least you are on your way. You can't overcome the fear and raise your self-esteem if you don't start somewhere.

List an area in which you would like to feel better about yourself and raise your self-esteem. _____

Now, plot a course that would help you achieve your ultimate goal and make you feel better about yourself:

Step 1 _____

_____

_____

_____

Step 2 _____

_____

_____

_____

Step 3 _____

_____

_____

_____

Step 4 _____

_____

_____

_____

Roadways to Increasing Your Self-Esteem

- **Get involved in your own life. Don't let others control you!!!**

    One of the easiest ways to maintain low self-esteem is to let other people rule your life. This gives you a sense of helplessness and them a sense of power. When you let other people constantly tell you what to do, you fail to realize your own potential, and your self-esteem suffers.

TIP: *To build high self-esteem, get involved in the decisions that affect your life. Take charge of your future. It is OK to listen to other people's advice, even to ask for their advice, but the decisions that you make should be your own.*

- **Take negative power away from your friends and family.**

Many times, you allow other people to create problems and cause your self-esteem to be lowered. You allow them to constantly belittle you, criticize you, and sometimes, you join in on the criticism of yourself. Nothing healthy can come from this behavior.

TIP: *Admit your shortcomings to yourself and tell yourself that you are working on correcting them. If you already know your weaknesses, no one can ever make you feel bad by pointing them out to you. Using this method allows you to take negative power away from those who would hurt you with words.*

- **Embrace the notion: "I am responsible for my own life."**

When you turn away from your responsibilities and duties in life, you weaken your worth and self-respect. Many times you do not lay claim to your successes or your failures. When you learn to admit your mistakes, combat your weaknesses, and tell yourself "I am responsible for me," you begin to build your self-esteem.

TIP: *Identify an area of your life where you have not taken responsibility, such as your school work, your family chores, or your social duties. Begin to develop a plan or set a goal (see Chapter 2) to assume responsibility for your past, your present, and most importantly, your future.*

- **Focus on your potential and your strengths.**

So often, you spend your time worrying about what you cannot do and not enough time celebrating your accomplishments and strengths. You beat yourself over the head each time you do not meet a goal or a deadline, but you never pat yourself on the back when you achieve a goal.

TIP: *Make a list of all the positive things that you know about yourself. "I am smart." "I am a friendly person." "I love my family." "I am a responsible person." Then, post these qualities on your bathroom or bedroom mirror so that you will be able to see them each day. Celebrate your accomplishments in life! Celebrate!*

- **Control your "self-talk"**

    "Self-talk" is the little voice you hear inside of your head throughout the day. This little voice may very seldom speak positively. Most of the time, the self-talk voice is telling you things like, "You're not good enough for that job," "You'll never pass that test," "You're not as smart as Janice," or "John always looks better than you do." Self-talk can be one of the most damaging aspects of your life.

    TIP: The next time you hear that little voice go off in your head, make an effort to stop it before it can finish its sentence. Make it a point to mentally say to the little voice, "I am good enough for that job," "I will pass this test," or "I am a nice and caring person." When you learn to control your self-talk, you begin to be one of your own best friends; positive self-esteem will follow.

- **Take at least one positive risk per week.**

    So often, you shield yourself from the unknown or from things you fear. This robs you of your potential and steals your self-esteem. Risk taking is one of the most dangerous and one of the hardest things a person can do. However, risk taking is the *only* way to promote growth in your life. It makes you stronger and carries you further than your mind could have imagined. Risk taking builds character.

    TIP: Risk taking does not involve putting your life in danger. However, it does involve putting your "comfort zone" in danger. The next time you have the opportunity to do something exciting or new and your little voice (self-talk) begins to chatter negatively, take control of your future and growth and try this new adventure, despite your fear. Once the activity is complete, you will have grown, and the fear will not be as great the next time around.

- **Stop comparing yourself to other people!!**

    Sometimes, you spend your life trying to be as pretty as Judy, as handsome as Tyrone, as smart as Tinaka, or as outgoing as James. When you compare yourself to other people, you are telling yourself that you are not as good as they are and that you do not have as much worth as they do. In time, your little voice begins to believe this and soon, your self-talk reminds you of your "shortcomings" every time you see someone else.

    TIP: The next time you begin to compare another person's looks, intellect, personality, or wealth with yours, remember that every person is different and not all people come from the same background. Celebrate your accomplishments!!

■ **Develop a victory wall or a victory file**

Many times, you tend to take your accomplishments and hide them in a drawer. You put your certificates or letters of praise in a box and soon, you have forgotten a certain accomplishment. When friends send you nice cards of thanks or you receive letters from an old friend, you should keep them in a treasured place so you see them from time to time.

TIP: If you do not have a special place in your residence for cards, letters, certificates or diplomas/degrees, start one today. *When you receive a degree or diploma, a certificate or award of appreciation, frame it and hang it on your wall, or put it on your bookcase so that you can see it often. Start a victory file in a place where you keep good grades, compliments from teachers, cartoons that make you laugh, and cards that made you feel good. Then, if you have a bad day, go through the file and you'll be surprised how good you feel when you are finished.*

■ **Surround yourself with people who support you.**

All too often, you keep people in your life who pull you down. You may tell yourself, "I've been friends with Jane since grammar school; I can't stop being her friend." This is one of the most difficult decisions a person can make, but if Jane is pulling you down and constantly telling you that you are not worthy, Jane has no place in your life.

TIP: Send Jane (or anyone who pulls you down) packing!!! Surround yourself with people who are positive and who support you and your efforts. The smartest and happiest people in this world are those who surround themselves with smart and happy people. Chose your companions and friends carefully.

■ **Keep your promises and be loyal to friends, family and yourself!!!**

If you have ever had someone break a promise to you, then you know how it feels to have your loyalty betrayed. The most outstanding feature of a person's character is the ability to be loyal and to do what they agreed to do. Few things will make you feel better about yourself and build your self–image than being a loyal person. Keeping promises and being loyal are trademarks of friendship, maturity, and good citizenship.

TIP: If you say that you are going to do something, do it. *Always check to see if you have the time to do a favor before you say you can. If you can't help, tell them so and ask them to consider you again at a later time.*

- **Win with grace—lose with class.**

    Everyone loves a winner, but everyone also loves a person who can lose with class and dignity. On the other hand, no one loves a bragging winner or a moaning loser. If you are engaged in sports, debate, acting, art shows, math competitions, academic teams, or talent shows, you will encounter winning and losing. We've all heard the old expression, "It's not if you win or lose, but how you play the game." This is one of the hardest things by which to live.

    TIP: If you win a show or event, be graceful and tactful. Do not brag to the loser and make them feel worse. This will lower your self-esteem and make you feel bad in the long run. You should always be proud of your accomplishments, but you should never let your win overshadow the healthy art of competition. You should always congratulate your opponents and tell them that you are happy to have had the honor to compete with them. If you lose, this does not mean that you were bad or the worst of them all. It simply means that you had more courage than the 50% of the population who would never have tried at all. If you lose, you should never belittle or degrade your opponents. People admire and respect people who can win or lose with grace and style.

- **Learn from your mistakes and move on!**

    A major sign of maturity and high self-esteem is the ability to admit your shortcomings and mistakes. Part of being human is making mistakes, but few of us know how to admit it when it happens. The most mature people and healthy people are those who have learned that mistakes are always going to happen, and the best way to deal with them is to admit them, correct what can be corrected, apologize if someone was hurt, and move on!

    TIP: When you make a mistake, never try to blame it on someone else. This can cause your self-esteem to fall. Mature people have learned how to take the heat for things they do. Always accept responsibility for your actions and decisions. Never try to overlook a mistake. When you make one, deal with it immediately before it grows into something uncontrollable. Putting off the decision to deal with a mistake only makes it worse. Never take pleasure in calling attention to other's mistakes. If you notice that someone has made an error, show them what is wrong and move on. *Never use this as an opportunity to get the upper hand. Remember, you are human, too, and you will make mistakes again. Above all, learn from your mistakes. A mistake made over and over, again and again, is not a mistake but a lesson never learned.*

- **See yourself as successful!!**

Just as you need a road map to get to places you've never been, the same is true of your life. You can't be successful if you do not plan your journey and then convince yourself that you will *get there*. You must see yourself as a success before you will ever be one.

TIP: Write your goals and objectives on a note card. Post these note cards in your car, on your mirror, on the front of your note books—anywhere where you can see them. Beyond writing your goals, you must state them as if they are already true. If your goal is to get a good-paying job, your note card might read, "I make $30,000 a year." If your goal is to lose weight, your card might read, "I weigh 120 pounds." This type of statement allows your mind to begin to see the positive effects of your efforts.

We are always getting ready to live, but never living.

R. W. Emerson, poet

Observations: Charting Your Course, Looking Beyond, Your Next Step

never let anyone put a price tag on you. You are worth more than money, more than drugs, more than cars, and you are worth much more than you probably give yourself credit. Many times, you are your own worst enemy and your own worst critic. It is time to start thinking positively about your life and your future. We have all made mistakes and messed things up, sometimes very badly, but as the famous actress Mary Pickford once said, "You can have a fresh start at any point that you please. And suppose that you have tried and tried again and failed and failed again . . . . There is always another chance for you . . . anytime that you choose it."

Choose happiness. Choose success. Choose tomorrow. Choose life. Choose to treat others with kindness. Choose to treat yourself with respect. Choose to be the best person you can be. With this motto, you will realize your potential and your self-esteem will blossom.

As a Result of this Chapter, and in Preparing for My Journey, I Plan to . . .

CHAPTER 2

Mapping Your Journey
Goal Setting and Motivation

CHAPTER 2

Far better is it to dare mighty things, to win glorious triumphs even though checkered with failure, than to take rank with those poor spirits who do not enjoy much nor suffer much because they live in the grey twilight that knows not victory nor defeat.
F. D. Roosevelt, U.S. President

In the earlier part of this century, a friend's grandfather came to America from Europe. He arrived by ship in the harbor of New York, passing by the Statue of Liberty. After being processed at Ellis Island, he went into a cafeteria in New York City to get something to eat. He sat down at an empty table and waited for someone to take his order. Of course, nobody ever came to his table. Finally, a man with a tray full of food sat down opposite him and told him how things worked in a cafeteria setting. "Start at the end of the line," he said to the old man, "and just go along and pick out what you want. At the end of the line, they'll tell you how much you have to pay for it."

"I soon learned that's how everything works in America," Grandpa told his friend. "Life is a cafeteria here. You can get anything you want as long as you're willing to pay the price. You can even get success. But you'll never get it if you sit at a table and wait for someone to bring it to you. You have to get up and get it yourself."

from Bits and Pieces
(V–N No. 1)

Shakespeare, a famous English playwright and poet, once said that "nothing will come of nothing." This statement rings true, doesn't it? If there are no plans, there will be no action. If there is no action, there can be no success. This chapter is intended to help you visualize the places where you hope to be in one, five, and even ten years. The exercises in this section are designed to examine your abilities in goal setting and determining your motivational level. Many people in this world have plans and goals, but they do not have the most important thing for achieving success: they do not have any objectives for reaching their goals and they do not have any motivation.

At the end of this chapter, you will be to

- Identify your fears that could hinder you in reaching your goals
- Define internal motivation
- Define external motivation
- Define long-term goals
- Define short-term goals

- Write a long-term goal
- Write a short-term goal
- Write an objective
- Identify barriers that destroy goals and decrease motivation

In the next exercise, take a moment and determine where you stand in relation to goal setting and motivation. Circle each answer that most closely matches your feelings about goals, motivation and personal responsibility.

SELF-STUDY

5=Strongly Agree
4=Agree
3=Don't Know
2=Disagree
1=Strongly Disagree

1. I use goals to guide my actions.   *1 2 3 4 5*
2. Goals are important to me.   *1 2 3 4 5*
3. I often set goals   *1 2 3 4 5*
4. I write objectives to my goals.   *1 2 3 4 5*
5. I face my fears head-on.   *1 2 3 4 5*
6. I take responsibility for my life.   *1 2 3 4 5*
7. I know where I want to be in five years.   *1 2 3 4 5*
8. Having more than one goal is important to me.   *1 2 3 4 5*
9. When I reached a goal, I celebrate.   *1 2 3 4 5*
10. I internalize my goals   *1 2 3 4 5*

TOTAL YOUR POINTS from these ten questions. Refer to the following rating scale to determine where you stand in relation to setting goals and developing motivation.

0–10   *You do not set goals and probably take little responsibility for your life. Your motivation level is low.*

11–20   *You probably know how to set goals, but you do not do so very often. You do not work toward reaching a goal.*

21–30   *You have average goal-setting and motivational skills. You know how to set goals, but lack a degree of motivation.*

31–40   *Your goal-setting skills are above average and you know how to reach your goals through motivation.*

41–50   *Your goal-setting skills, objective-writing, and motivational skills are excellent.*

Does your score match how you personally feel about your goal setting and motivational abilities? Why or why not? If your score is lower than you would like for it to be, this chapter will assist you in learning how to write goals, set objectives, and develop motivation.

What Do These People Have in Common?

Albert Einstein was four years old before he could speak and seven before he could read a word.

A newspaper fired **Walt Disney** because he had "no good ideas."

Lorraine Hansberry was raised in a very poor, run–down side of Chicago as a young child. She and her family later moved to an upper-class white neighborhood when she was in her teens. She and her family were threatened and called names. Lorraine was almost killed by a concrete slab that was thrown through her window by an angry mob who did not want her family to live in the neighborhood. As a playwright, she went on to become the first African-American woman to have a Broadway show (*A Raisin in the Sun*) and the first African-American woman to ever win the New York Drama Critics Circle Award.

Abraham Lincoln dropped out of grade school, ran a country store and went broke, took fifteen years to pay off his bills, lost a race for the state legislature at 32, failed in a second business, ran for the State House, lost twice, ran for the Senate, lost twice, finally ran for president and won, but was hated by half of the country. Eventually, he became one of the most famous leaders of the world.

Winston Churchill was a poor student who stuttered. He won a Nobel Prize at the age of 24 and became one of the most powerful leaders and speakers in the world.

Malcolm X was abandoned as a child, was very poor, and spent time in prison as a young adult. He later became one of the most powerful speakers and leaders for the Civil Rights Movements of the 1960s.

So, what did these people have in common? Luck? A tooth fairy? A genie in a lamp? No. They had . . .

GOALS! OBJECTIVES! MOTIVATION!

"Come to the edge,"

he said.

They said, "we are afraid."

"Come to the edge,"

he said.

They came.

He pushed them . . .

and they flew.

Guillaume Apollinaire

Eliminating Fear

TWO FEARS THAT HINDER GROWTH AND STIFLE MOTIVATION

The Fear of Failure
The Fear of Change

Beginning your journey means realizing that every fear you have is learned. That's right, learned! You are born with only two fears: the fear of loud noises and the fear of falling. The rest are learned. Many times, your progress and success are limited because you are afraid to move forward, afraid to take chances, or you are afraid to set goals beyond what you already know how to do.

Every person has a comfort zone. You can say that the comfort zone is the "little box" in which you live and feel safe. This is the small space where you feel comfortable and secure. The reason for goal setting, writing objectives, and developing motivation is to *expand* your comfort zone so that you will feel safe and secure in more activities, with more people, doing more things, and traveling to more places. Vincent Van Gogh, a famous artist, once said, "The best way to know life is to love many things." The best way to love many things, and in the end, know life better, is to take chances, set goals, be motivated, and *expand* your comfort zone.

This sounds easy, doesn't it? Actually, many people have goals, but they are afraid to move forward or they do not know how to move forward. Often, your fears rest on very weak ground. If you examine why you are afraid to leave your comfort zone, you realize that the reasons are simple, and the solutions to these fears can be even more simple.

The first fear that you will want to conquer is the fear of failure. Goals are meaningless if you are afraid to go after them. Many times, you may have said to yourself, "I could never do that; I'd fail and I don't want to fail." Now you have to ask yourself, is it better to try and fail or never to try at all? The answer, once again, is quite simple. You know in your mind that it is always better to try and fail than never to try at all. Think about where our civilization would be if we had been afraid to deal with fire, afraid to build the first town, afraid to fly, or afraid to build a building with more than one story. Failure is a part of growth.

Think about it—you learn a great deal from your failures, don't you? Remember when you were young and you tried to ride your bicycle for the first time without training wheels. It was scary and you probably wrecked a few times before you were able to ride with a great deal of success. But you overcame your fear and learned how to ride without training wheels. You mastered your fear.

Some of your strength comes from difficult situations in which your comfort zones were stretched. It is a guarantee that if you take chances beyond your comfort zone, you may get knocked down a few times. You may have a few failures. We've all been there, haven't we? However, it is also a guarantee that if you do not take chances beyond your comfort zone, you may not grow. Remember the old saying, "That which does not kill us, makes us stronger."

The fear of change is another thing that can rob you of your hopes and dreams. Humans are creatures of habit, and in that light, change is neither natural nor desired. Change causes a great deal of frustration and physical reaction. Change can make you feel nervous, tense, afraid, guilty, tired, depressed, and even angry. However, when planning your goals, it is helpful to realize that change is the only thing in this world that is guaranteed. You can't stop it. The most successful people in this world are the people who have learned how to deal with change and accept it as a part of life.

Just as change can be frustrating and trying, change can also be exciting and rewarding. Change keeps us alive. In order to learn how to communicate with new people, feel comfortable in new situations, and develop new ideas, change must occur. In order to deal with change, you should remember:

Change is never easy

Change is almost always met with resistance

The person who brings about change is usually not liked very well

Change creates unfamiliar ground

Change takes courage

In the following questions, take a moment and reflect on your life and what situations cause you fear and possibly hinder you from growth.

1. List five activities that you feel comfortable doing.

1. _____
2. _____
3. _____
4. _____
5. _____

2. List three activities that you would like to do, but are afraid to try. Explain why you are afraid to try them. Explain what would encourage you to do this activity.

1. _____

I am afraid because _____
_____

What would make you do this activity? _____
_____

2. _____

I am afraid because _____
_____

What would make you do this activity? _____
_____

3. _____

I am afraid because _____
_____

What would make you do this activity? _____
_____

3. List three people with whom you feel comfortable. Tell why.

1. _____
Why? _____
_____

2. _____
Why? _____
_____

3. _____
Why? _____
_____

4. List three people with whom you would not feel comfortable. Tell why you are uncomfortable and what it would take to make you spend time with them.

1. _____
Why? _____
_____

What would make you spend time? _____
_____

2. _____
Why? _____
_____

What would make you spend time? _____
_____

3. _____
Why? _____
_____

What would make you spend time? _____
_____

GOAL SETTING AND MOTIVATION

Review your answers. If you spend some time reviewing your responses to questions 2 and 4, you will find that your fears are probably rooted in family traditions or that you could not come up with many reasons. You may have even written statements like, "I've never done it before" or "I just don't know them very well."

A major part of your education is learning how to expand your horizons through people, places, and things with which you are not familiar. Fear can play a major roll in keeping your comfort zone small and stagnant.

- Don't be afraid to fail.
- Don't be afraid to change.
- Don't be afraid to take chances.
- Don't be afraid to go beyond what you know and feel at this moment.

You'll be amazed at how quickly your comfort zone will grow once you overcome your fears and learn how to set goals, and discover your motivation.

DON'T BE AFRAID TO FAIL

You've failed many times, although you may not remember. You fell down the first time you tried to walk. You almost drowned the first time you tried to swim, didn't you? Did you hit the ball the first time you swung a bat? Heavy hitters, the ones who hit the most home runs, also strike out a lot.

R.H. Macy
failed seven times
before his store in New York
caught on.
English novelist, John Casey,
got 753 rejection slips
before he published 564 books.
Babe Ruth struck out 1,330 times,
but he also hit
714 home runs.
Don't worry about
failure.
Worry about the
chances you miss
when you don't even try.

Author Unknown

What Is a Goal?

ebster's New Collegiate Dictionary defines a goal as "the end toward which effort is directed." Have you ever wanted a new car, a CD player, or a new outfit? If you have, then you have had a goal—the goal of getting one or all of these physical material things. Goals are simply what you want and what you are willing to do to get them.

There are two types of goals that we must discuss; obtainable and unobtainable. We can also call these goals realistic and unrealistic. The obtainable or realistic goal is well defined, well planned, and well organized, and a map is laid to reach that goal. The unobtainable or unrealistic goal is one that is not clearly defined, is open ended, poorly organized, and no map exists to reach the goal. It is a goal that you might say you want, but one to which you have not committed yourself to achieving. In other words, you have not developed a plan to reach this goal.

Goals also have time-lines. You can have short-term goals and long-term goals. Short-term goals may be things such as:

- I want to purchase a new CD player.
- I want to make an A on my next English test.

Long-term goals will be more elaborate and planned:

- I want to be a doctor.
- I want to get married and have three children.

Both long-term and short-term goals are important. Today's generation has been accused of having no long-term goals. "They want it and they want it now," we've heard others say. Goals take sacrifice, planning, and a great deal of hard work; without goals, your life becomes meaningless. A popular athletic ad states, "No Pain, No Gain!" In other words, if you do not set your goals, sacrifice what is needed to achieve them, and then work hard, there will be no gain.

You are never given a wish without the power to make it come true.

Unknown

Why Are Goals Important?

How do you feel about goal setting? Studies, research, professionals, friends, family, and foes will tell you that goals are one of the most important aspects of life. But why? Why must you have them? Why are they so important? Perhaps no where can you find a more powerful answer than that given in a study conducted in 1953 by Yale University. While the study is older, it is important to look at it because it reveals a very important fact about goal setting.

A survey was given to the senior class. They were asked several questions, and three of those questions dealt with goals. The questions were "Have you set goals?" "Have you written them down?" and "Do you have a plan to accomplish these goals?" Very few seniors answered yes to these questions (only about 3% of the entire senior class).

Twenty years later, the living seniors of this class were surveyed again. The research told Yale University that the 3% of the class who set goals were happier and more successful than those who did not have goals. However, the most astonishing fact was that the 3% who

set goals had 97% of all the wealth of the entire class. In other words, these 3% of goal setters were more wealthy than the entire rest of the class combined!!!! We do *not* want to suggest that money equals success; we do, however, want to suggest that setting goals, for any outcome, can lead to accomplishment.

GOALS WORK!

Types of Goals

Goals come in a variety of packages. There are as many goals as there are people who set them. People can have many goals in many different parts of their lives. Such goals may be in categories such as:

Social

Academic

Physical

Family

Financial

Some of the basic goals are listed here.

GOAL SETTING AND MOTIVATION   43

Social Goal:	I will learn how to meet new people by attending two school functions per month.
Academic Goal:	I will make an A on my research paper in History by doing the research early, writing a rough draft, and making an appointment with my instructor.
Physical Goal:	I will lose 25 pounds by December 31 by watching my fat grams and exercising.
Family Goal:	I will spend more time with my family by blocking out two Saturdays per month to all other activities.
Financial Goal:	I will save $1000 in one year by opening a savings account and contributing $19.23 per week.

Your goals do not have to fall into one of these categories. In addition to the goals listed, there could be spiritual goals, self-improvement goals, career goals, community service goals, artistic goals, and so on. The most important thing is that your goal should be your own; it should be internalized.

How to Write a Goal

Goal setting seems rather easy, doesn't it? Actually, it takes some time, thought and preparation for them to come true. An obtainable and realistic goal statement should have the following in order to work:

An action statement

Objectives

Target date (deadline)

Outcome statement

The goal must be one that can be measured. In other words, you must be able to prove that it was completed. For example:

GOAL 1 I will save **(the action statement)** $100 by putting back $10 a week **(the objective)**. I will have $100 dollars by January 31 **(target date)**.

Some goals will be more complicated and have more steps to complete. An example might be

GOAL 2   I will lose **(the action statement)** 25 pounds by December 31 **(target date)**.

Objectives

- Eat the proper number of calories
- Consume less fat
- Walk four miles five days per week

Both goals, however, are obtainable *and* measurable. You can measure them by having $100 in the bank and by using scales to weigh yourself.

Goals need to be written in a positive fashion, using action verbs. A poorly written goal might read as such:

I want to try to lose ten or fifteen pounds this summer.

This goal will never be obtained. Why? It has no purpose, it has no action, it has no target date, and it has no objectives.

Finally you need to write an outcome statement in reference to your goal. An outcome statement will describe what your life will be like once the goal has been reached.

OUTCOME STATEMENT

When I save $100 dollars, I will be able to buy two new CDs and a great pair of running shoes. I will be able to enjoy the music and exercise in my new shoes.

The outcome statement allows you to visualize your life once the goal has been accomplished.

What Is an Objective?

Objectives can be called the road map to achieving a goal. They are the strategic plans by which you can get the new CD player, the new wardrobe, or the new car. They are the means by which you can graduate from college.

Let's look at several goals and work through a few objectives for achieving the goal.

SHORT-TERM GOAL

Goal: I want to purchase a new CD player.

Objective(s):
1. Find a part-time job
2. Save $10 a week
3. Save my income tax return with the bank balance
4. Shop around for the most inexpensive CD player
5. Buy the CD player

LONG-TERM GOAL

Goal: I want to be a nurse.

Objective(s):
1. Enroll in allied health degree program
2. Study at least three hours per night
3. Maintain at least a 3.5 GPA
4. Complete my degree
5. Do internship
6. Pass all federal and state boards
7. Begin to practice nursing as a profession

While some of your goals may not be this big, all goals require objectives and plans. CD players are never purchased and nurses never practice without goal setting, planning, sacrifice, and hard work.

Roadblocks to Success: Barriers to Achieving Your Goals

Regardless of how hard we try, how much we struggle, how many objectives we plan, there are going to be times when roadblocks or speed bumps arise that threaten to destroy our goals and motivation. Create a list of barriers that could possibly keep you from achieving your goals.

1. _____
2. _____
3. _____
4. _____
5. _____

You may have listed things like money, time, family, transportation, child care, lack of basic skills, peer pressure, alcohol or drug addiction, or lack of motivation.

Using this list, talk with the group assigned by your professor and create some ideas of where you could go to find assistance in overcoming these barriers. Often, we can easily point out to ourselves and others why we *cannot* do something, but seldom do we take the time to try to resolve the problems and eliminate the barrier. This exercise will give you a good idea of college and community resources that can assist you in overcoming your barriers.

1. I can find help _____
2. I can find help _____
3. I can find help _____
4. I can find help _____
5. I can find help _____

You may have listed some of the places identified in the block below. Review this list because it may give you some ideas of where to find help that you and your group may not have thought about.

CAMPUS AND COMMUNITY RESOURCES

Financial Aid Office

Veteran's Office

Mature Student (Non-Traditional) Services

Minority Student Services

Disabled Student Services

Career Counseling Office

Academic Assistance Center

Peer Tutoring Center

Computer Assistance Center

Nothing in this world can take the place of persistence. Talent will not; nothing is more common than unsuccessful people with talent. Genius will not; unrewarded genius is almost a proverb. Education will not; the world is full of educated derelicts. Persistence and determination alone are eternal. The slogan "press on" has solved and always will solve the problems of the human race.

Calvin Coolidge, U.S. President

Personal Counseling Center

Campus Religious Organization

Student Organizations

Hall or Residence Counselors

Professors

Staff Members

The Library

Community Drug and Alcohol Center

Campus Health Services

Community Organizations

Churches, Synagogues, Mosques, Temples

Family and Friends

Old High School Teacher or Counselors

Traveling the Road on Your Own: Motivation

What Is Motivation?

Motivation is a *force*, the driving force that causes you to do something—to act! Without motivation, you achieve very little. You can have all the goals and objectives in the world, but without motivation, very little will ever happen. You not only have to write goals and set objectives, but you have to work at becoming a motivated person. You have to actually do something with your plans and goals.

> "It ain't enough to get the breaks, you gotta be willing to use 'em."
>
> ***Long***

Why Is Motivation Important?

For many of you, this is the first time in your life that you are on your own. It may be a strange experience for some of you. For others, it may be one of the most exciting things you have ever done. You may be living at school, some of you may be living in an off–campus apartment and some of you may have a home of your own. For others, you may have your first full–time or part–time job. Many of you have families, relationships and outside commitments, *and* go to school full time. For some students, this may be the first time that you have left your child and spouse in the care of someone else. For most students today, there are many things "pulling" at you from many directions.

At this point in your life, there may be many people pulling at you but no one *pushing* you. No one to wake you up and put you on a bus or drag you to the car so that you can make it on time. If you go to class—fine. If you don't go to class—that's OK, too! You will have some teachers who do not care if you are there or not. You will have some teachers who never take attendance. It may be that you are in a class so large that your name is never known by the instructor. More often than not, however, your professors *will* care if you come to class, many professors *do* take class roll, and lots of professors, regardless of the size of the class, *know* your name. So, it is very important that you not adopt the attitude that it is OK not to attend class. The motivation to go to class and do well in college will have to come from within.

List the things that motivate you in your life; in other words, what pushes you?

_____

_____

_____

_____

_____

_____

_____

You may have listed such things as

Money

Family

Friends

Learning

The most important step in goal setting and objective writing is to determine if your goals and objectives are internal or external.

INTERNAL (VS.) EXTERNAL GOALS AND MOTIVATION

Internal (adjective)	Existing within the limits or surface of something; situated inside of the body.
External (adjective)	Having the outward appearance of something; situated outside of the body.

There comes a point when you have to stop, take a moment, reflect, and ask yourself, "Am I doing this for myself or for someone else?" When you are setting goals, striving to find the motivation, or simply stepping along from day to day, you should develop a clear picture of what you want, why you want it, and *why* you are doing this act to get it. In other words, "Why are you in college?" Why are you working at that job of yours?" So often, you push yourself from day to day feeling unhappy, unsatisfied, frustrated, and even angry for having to do certain things. Usually, you are most unhappy or unsatisfied when you are doing something that you do not enjoy or something that someone is making you do.

Realizing that every person must do certain things that are unpleasant or not fulfilling is the first step in finding motivation. However, the happiest person in the world is one who has discovered how to internalize these unpleasant tasks and set additional goals based on internal motivation.

Example: When Ben was going to college, he had to pay all of his tuition. His parents were not able to assist him. He worked in a factory for seven years while working his way through his bachelor's and master's degrees. However, there were two summers between his sophomore and junior years when he found an additional part-time job with a local sewer district. The hourly pay rate was the highest he had ever made in his life at that time. However, you can imagine how he hated that job. Hot! Nasty! Horrible odors! Disgusting! He dreaded getting up each morning because he knew what the day would hold. He worked in the sewers from 8 AM until 2 PM and then went to work in the factory from 4 PM until 12 midnight. Not an easy or satisfying life.

It was during this time in his life that he learned how to internalize this activity and look at it as a stepping stone. Soon, his bank account grew, he was able to pay off his used car, and finally, he saw enough money in his account to pay for his fall and spring tuitions!

The days of working in the sewer and the mill were not as hard for him because he internalized his goals. He saw it as an opportunity to get what he eventually wanted, not as a horrible life unfit for living. He began to work for his future and not look at each day as a tragedy. He embraced the fact that he had a job that paid well and that he would use this job to make a better life for himself and his family. He internalized the goal.

Had Ben looked at this time in his life as just a job, he would have never been able to live through it. He often said that he would have quit the sewer job and would have left the mill shortly thereafter had he not internalized those tasks. In quitting, however, he would have robbed himself of a college education. When he internalized this job and looked at it in the perspective of his future, it made the situation bearable.

This is how you should look at your daily tasks that are unpleasant or boring and how you must set your goals. You should look at them in terms of the end result—what you eventually want. Internalizing your goals will help you develop motivation and eventually reach your goal.

From the list that you generated earlier, divide your motivators into

INTERNAL MOTIVATORS   **EXTERNAL MOTIVATORS**

_____   _____

_____   _____

_____   _____

_____   _____

After discussing goal setting, objectives, roadblocks, and motivation, you are ready to begin planning a goal and working toward it. Next, you will find a goal-setting worksheet that will assist you in plotting your course and setting goals. Use this sheet to set goals you *actually* want to achieve, not just a classroom project. When you plan your goals on this sheet, you should copy them and post them in a place where you can see them every day.

ROADWAYS TO REACHING YOUR GOALS

- **Carefully examine your life to determine what you really want.**
- **Seek advice from people who have achieved your goal. Ask them how they got it and if it was worth going through what they had to endure.**
- **Set your goals high, but be realistic.**
- **Set attainable goals.**
- **Set goals that can be measured.**
- **Set both long- and short-term goals.**
- **Develop a plan to achieve your goals, in other words, objectives.**
- **Write clear objectives that can be reached in steps.**
- **Look at your goals and objectives as one step at a time.**
- **Internalize your goals so that they become your own.**
- **Find something that motivates you and stick with it.**

- Tell people about your goals and ask for their help in reaching them.

- Don't let setbacks cripple you. Look at it as a lesson and *move on*.

- Don't let others dictate your goals to you. Set your own goals.

- Write your goals and objectives down and place them where you can see them every day of your life.

- Think positively. Good things come to those who wait—and work hard.

Goal-Setting Worksheet

Write a goal that you have:
Goal: _____
_____
_____

Why is the goal important? _____
_____
_____

Now, map out a way to achieve that goal. What are your objectives?
_____
_____
_____
_____
_____

Target Date _____
Outcome Statement _____

Barriers to overcome _____
_____
_____

■ WRITE A SHORT-TERM GOAL

_____
_____
_____

Why is the goal important to you? _____
_____
_____

List the objectives: _____
_____
_____
_____

Target Date _____
Outcome Statement _____
_____
_____
_____

Barriers to overcome _____
_____
_____

■ WRITE A LONG-TERM GOAL

_____
_____

_____
_____

Why is the goal important to you? _____
_____
_____
_____

List the objectives:
_____
_____
_____
_____
_____

Target Date _____
Outcome Statement _____
_____
_____

Barriers to overcome _____
_____
_____

Observations

The remaining chapters in this book will be useless to you if you have not mastered the art of goal setting, objective writing, and motivation building. The most important aspect of this chapter is that it can't really be taught to you. Your instructor can show you how to write a goal, how to construct an objective list, but beyond that, your instructor has no control or power. **You Are In Control!!!**

No one can write your goals for you. No one can live your life for you. No one can finish your education for you. No one can motivate you except yourself. Remember, "you are never given a wish without the power to make it come true."

As a Result of this Chapter, and in Preparing for My Journey, I Plan to . . .

CHAPTER 3

Planning to Reach Your Destination on Time

Time Management

CHAPTER 3

> Never before have we had so little time in which to do so much.
> *F. D. Roosevelt,*
> *U.S. President*

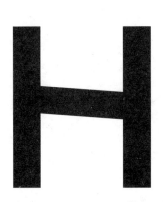

Her name was Alice. Alice was *always* late. Alice and I became friends during my sophomore year in college. She was a year ahead of me in school and was someone that I looked up to. Alice was involved in the Student Government as well as the Student Activity Programming Board. Initially, I just assumed that she had a lot of responsibility and was occasionally late.

Then, after getting to know Alice a little better, her "lateness" became more the rule than the exception. People kidded Alice about "always being late" and we made our jokes about her being "late for her own funeral." No one realized the seriousness of her chronic tardy behavior until one day when she confided to us that she had been late for a final exam in a class, and the instructor would not allow her to enter the room after the prescribed time. As a consequence, Alice failed her political science class, and it caused some major problems with her financial aid. The fact that Alice was always late finally caught up with her. Unfortunately, it cost her a great deal in terms of financial aid dollars and in time spent in repeating Political Science 101.

The management of your time, the act of getting things done, seems to confuse students that have not yet mastered the technique of time management. Do you feel that you are a successful time manager? Do you keep to-do lists or have a calendar that you regularly depend on? The process of time management can be quite simple, yet, if undeveloped, can cause major problems.

This chapter is designed to help you learn to manage your time more effectively. After reading this chapter and completing the exercises, you should be able to

- Understand that there are different kinds of time
- Understand how time passes
- Be able to keep a time log and then analyze the log to determine where your time goes
- Understand how time management systems can help you become a better student
- Be able to develop a study plan based on your own time analysis.

TODAY		Date	Jan. 25
List of Priorities		Appointments and Classes	
Priority Code		End-of-Day Checklist	
3	Buy Mom's Gift	8:00	Math Class
3	Wash Car	9:00	History Class
1	Study - French Test	✓ 10:15	Student Gv. Mtg.
1	Exchange Work Hours	✓ 11:30	Canteen w/ John
2	Run 3 Miles	12:30	Lunch w/ Rolanda
1	Read Ch.14	✓ 2:00	Study
2	Write 2/15 Paper	5 - 6	Run w/ Rolanda
Expenses for Today		Phone Numbers Needed Today	
lunch - 2.50 gas - 5.00 notebook - 3.79		Mary - 555 -1234	
Fun Breaks			
Canteen @ 11:30 w/ John		Run w/ Rolanda	
Sacred Day to Look Forward to: Ski Trip !! Feb. 18			

Time Analysis

Time is the scarcest resource and unless it is managed, nothing else can be managed.

Peter Drucker

How well do you manage your time? Before you begin this chapter, be honest with yourself and write, in the space provided, how successful you see yourself as a time manager and why:

_____
_____
_____
_____
_____

Was your response a positive or negative one? If it was negative, you may be able to change. Take a second look at the suggestions in this chapter and give them a try; you have nothing to lose—and everything to gain. At least give this information an opportunity to work for you. If it was a positive response, you, too, can benefit from the exercises and information in this chapter. This chapter could reinforce and verify what you already know how to do.

One way to analyze how you view time is to complete the following Self-Study. You will find ten questions in the exercise that relate to your own opinion of time management. Take a moment and rate each statement truthfully. Spend some time and think about each statement carefully.

SELF-STUDY

1. I know how to prioritize my responsibilities.
   1 2 3 4 5

2. I manage my time efficiently.
   1 2 3 4 5

3. Completing daily goals is important to me.
   1 2 3 4 5

4. Making a daily to-do list is necessary for me.
   1 2 3 4 5

5. Writing down all of my assignments helps me.
   1 2 3 4 5

6. I use short- and long-term planning.
   1 2 3 4 5

7. I understand system- and non-system-imposed time.
   1 2 3 4 5

8. My friends control my time.
   1 2 3 4 5

9. I am in control of my time.
   1 2 3 4 5

10. I understand that time management helps me to become a better student.
    1 2 3 4 5

5=Strongly Agree

4=Agree

3=Don't Know

2=Disagree

1=Strongly Disagree

TOTAL YOUR POINTS from these ten questions. Refer to the following rating scale to determine where you stand in relation to dealing with time management.

0–10   *You give very little thought to time management in your life and probably run late, procrastinate, and are late turning in assignments.*

11–20   *You don't give a great deal of thought to time management. You turn in some things on time, but probably rush to get them done at the very last minute.*

21–30   *Your time management skills are average. You plan ahead, but sometimes, you do not follow your time management plan.*

31–40   *You are a good time manager. You make a plan, and most of the time, you stick to that plan. You turn in your assignments on time and usually do not procrastinate.*

41–50   *Your time management skills are excellent. You develop a time management plan, stick to it, and do not procrastinate. If an assignment is ever late, there has been some unforeseen circumstance to make that happen.*

TIME MANAGEMENT

Do your score and the rating scale match what you feel about your time management skills? If not, don't worry. If you read this chapter carefully and complete the exercises within, your time management skills will be enhanced.

FACTS ABOUT TIME

There are several statements about time that apply to everyone. A few of the statements may not seem to apply to you, but think about each one individually.

- Few people have enough time, yet everyone has all there is.

- Every man and woman has 24 hours each day, 168 hours each week, 52 weeks per year—no more, no less; the time you are able control should be the area of time management you are most concerned about.

- Time cannot be accumulated or stockpiled. It flows at a fixed rate.

- The real problem is not *with* time, but what *you* choose to do with the time that you have available to manage.

The last fact of time presented, the notion that you choose the activity that uses your time, is quite important. You are in charge of a large percentage of your time, and it is a choice that you make that determines how productive that time is going to be. At times, you've probably felt as if you were not in control; everyone experiences this feeling at some point in their life. The real key is that you *can* control time that is not typically used for school, work, or commuting. You will, no doubt, need to take into account and schedule appropriate time for sleeping and eating. Other than that, your time can be divided into two categories.

DIFFERENT TYPES OF TIME

System-Imposed Time: the time that you spend in class, at work or at other regularly scheduled times. You can't do much about this time except by getting out of the "system."

Non-System-Imposed Time: basically, your free time. This includes time not spent in class or at work. *This is your time.* This is time that you control. *You* are in charge here.

The fact of the matter is that you can do little about controlling system-imposed time, other than removing yourself from the system. You, however, have made the decision to pursue your education, and with that decision comes certain expectations. Attending class, participating in activities, socializing, and working will be a part of your daily life. Successful students must accept the circumstances and demands of college and outside activities and learn how to control or manage their time.

Non-system-imposed time, and the choices we make about how to spend free time, can also determine how successful we are. Basically, it all can be summarized by talking about priorities. Priorities are adopted after certain goals have been established. For example, if we have determined that buying a new car is a goal, then getting to work, doing a good job (so that we will not be fired), and earning money are all priorities. If your goal is to complete your education, placing a high priority on study time or time outside the classroom preparing for the next class should be a priority.

If this is confusing to you, here is another way to think about time. System-imposed time is required time; you *must* sleep a certain number of hours to remain healthy. It is required time for your body that you cannot avoid. Non-system-imposed time is free time; what you choose to do with your free time is your choice. This is time that *you* decide how to spend.

TIME MANAGEMENT

List some system-imposed activities that you are involved in this semester:

_____
_____
_____
_____

Can you change any of these activities? _____

How would you change these activities? _____
_____
_____
_____

List some non-system-imposed activities in which you are involved:

_____
_____
_____
_____

Are they helping you in college? _____

Why or why not? _____

Should these activities be changed? _____

How? _____
_____
_____
_____

I'd love to help you, but

I haven't time—

I can't accept, having

no time—

I can't think, I can't

read, I'm swamped, I

haven't time—

I'd like to pray, but I

haven't time.

Michael Queist

Understanding How Time Passes

Remember the old saying "A watched pot never boils?" How often have you been waiting for an event to occur and could swear that you had waited an hour, only to find out that you had waited only ten or fifteen minutes? Our perception or understanding of how time passes influences how we ultimately utilize our time. Are you guilty of setting your watch or clock ahead five, ten, or even fifteen minutes? If you are, you are probably attempting to "buy" time. Later on in this chapter, we will discover why this does not work and why you should not allow yourself to believe that you can buy time.

Now, let's begin testing our perception of time. For the next activity, you will need to put all watches, clocks, or other time pieces away. Your instructor will help you with this activity. When your instructor gives you the proper sign, close your eyes, relax, and just sit back for a while. In a little while, the instructor will ask you to open your eyes.

Answer the professor's question in this blank: _____
_____

What is the correct answer? _____
Was your estimate more or less? _____
What does that say about your perception of the passage of time? _____
_____
_____

Did this surprise you? Why or why not? _____
_____
_____

Write your observations about your perception of time in the space below:
_____
_____
_____
_____

Putting Real Time to Work

Now, let's put some of this to work in a real-life situation. Imagine that you have the following tasks to accomplish. Arrange these tasks in the order by which you get them all done in the least amount of time.

_____ A. Pick up parcel. It is heavy. The place closes at 11 AM.

_____ B. Buy frozen food for the evening's dinner.

_____ C. You have no cash. You need money. You have no credit cards and cannot write a check. Go to bank.

_____ D. Your car is almost out of gas. Go to gas station.

_____ E. Your child is sick and you need to get medication from the pharmacy before going to school.

_____ F. Class begins at noon. You need to review previous lecture notes before walking in.

_____ G. Take frozen food and medicine home.

What did this process teach you? Did you learn anything about priorities? How do you normally prioritize your day? _____
_____
_____

Where Does Your Time Go?

At the end of a busy day, have you ever looked back and wondered, "Where did my time go?" If you have, you are in the majority. A large percentage of our time escapes us, and we have no real idea of what we did with the time. Certainly we know that we have spent what seemed to be hours on the road, commuting to and from school, sports events for our children, studying, and work. But in order to help you get a handle on your time, realize where your time is going, and then begin to manage your time, you need to keep a log of *every* activity for a week. You will need to record in this log everything that must be done; this includes carpool, extracurricular activities, work, and so on. This is your first step. Pick what you would consider a normal week in terms of your schedule. Then—this part can be hard to do—on the chart provided, write down every activity you are involved in and give the exact time. Include routine items such as eating, sleeping, and so forth. (You may want to copy this form onto another sheet of paper so that you can carry it with you wherever you go.) Hopefully, at the end of the week, you will begin to see where pockets of time are located and begin to recognize system-imposed time and non-system-imposed time. You will hopefully begin to prioritize your tasks and then manage the remaining time to be a more productive student. Your time log need not be complicated; the important thing is that you stay with this project until the week is over. Then, and only then, can you begin to realize how your time is spent.

	SUN	MON	TUES	WED	THURS	FRI	SAT
6:00							
7:00							
8:00							
9:00							
10:00							
11:00							
12:00							
1:00							
2:00							
3:00							
4:00							
5:00							
6:00							
7:00							
8:00							
9:00							
10:00							
11:00							

Once you have completed at least two days on your time log, answer the following questions:

1. What am I doing that does not need to be done at all? _____

_____

_____

_____

2. *On what items am I spending too much time?* _____

_____

_____

_____

3. *On what items and I spending too little time?* _____

_____

_____

_____

4. *Does my schedule allow for flexibility?* _____

_____

_____

_____

5. *How can I change my time log to be able to fit in required items and still have time left over?* _____

_____

_____

_____

6. *How did you feel about keeping a time log?* _____

_____

_____

_____

By answering these six questions, you have begun to analyze how you "feel" about time management. Continue to keep the time log and at the end of the week, go back and answer these six questions again. These questions, along with the exercise, allow you to see where your time goes and where you are spending large amounts of time.

Your Study Time

The time spent studying needs to be time that you are physically and emotionally prepared. It is important that you are not tired or hungry. It is also important that you attempt to let go of distracting emotional issues. You will not be able to use your time wisely if you have not met the needs of your mind and body. (Another barrier that affects study time is procrastination. We will discuss that a little later on in the chapter.)

When choosing your study time, think about your peak times. If possible, select those times to study. For example, some students prefer to study during the early morning hours, whereas other students prefer evening hours.

As a student, you need to set aside a certain number of hours—five days a week—for studying. The amount of time spent will vary from day to day and from student to student. A general guide to go by is that for every hour spent in class, two hours should be spent studying for that class. For example, if your class meets three hours per week, then, you should spend six hours outside of class studying. This is a realistic amount of time and should be used as a guide. You should try to remember that some classes will require much more time; others not as much. Most students require one to three hours of outside time (per course, per week) to be academically successful.

Of the courses you are now taking, which ones will require more study time?

_____
_____

Why? _____
_____
_____

Which courses will require the least amount of outside study time? _____

_____
_____

Why? _____
_____
_____

This raises a good point for the nontraditional student. Is it realistic to be a full-time student, a full-time employee, and a parent? Students who find that they are able to juggle a variety of commitments will always tell you that it is not easy. Decisions, tough decisions, about what is most urgent and what can wait must be made on a daily basis. Many successful adult students also indicate that adequate support groups, either family, friends, or spouse, help tremendously with the time-management problem of being a student, an employee, and a parent. Try to remember that the decision to be a student is an important one, one that deserves adequate time.

Now, let's take some time to get a handle on your own situation. Use the following weekly time schedule to complete the following tasks:

1. Block out the time you are in class, at work, participating in religious/social activities, and so on.

2. Examine the time remaining, and indicate the time that could be used for studying.

	SUN	MON	TUES	WED	THURS	FRI	SAT
6:00							
7:00							
8:00							
9:00							
10:00							
11:00							
12:00							
1:00							
2:00							
3:00							
4:00							
5:00							
6:00							
7:00							
8:00							
9:00							
10:00							
11:00							

Are there chunks of time you can dedicate to studying? _____

If not, what can you eliminate? _____

_____

When do they exist during the day? _____

_____

After completing the study schedule, use the space provided to identify the things that might interfere with your study time. _____

_____

What do you think you could do to prevent these situations from interfering with your study time? _____

_____

_____

_____

There are some concrete things that you can do to be able to juggle your study time with your family responsibilities. A few suggestions:

- Schedule study time at a time when your school-age children are studying.

- Develop a network of other students with children. Trade sitting responsibility with the people in this network. Volunteer to sit with their children when they are studying, and ask them to sit with yours when you are preparing for a big test.

- Pre-determine what your peak study times will be for the semester, and ask family and other friends to help with babysitting responsibilities during these peak times.

Your Study Plan

Every night before you go to bed, make a to-do list for the next day to help you organize your study time. This plan should enable you to get the most from your valuable time. It is important to list first those assignments that are most difficult to complete. If you save those items until the end, you will not be at your best. This could increase your frustration, and you may decide not to complete the assignment. If there are unfinished tasks on your list, the unfinished work should be transferred to your study plan for the next day.

Take a look at the following example to see how a typical study plan may look. This example uses a prioritized list of things that must be done today: a 1 for the most critical and urgent, and a 2 or a 3 for less critical items. This system will work for you, and you may use anything as a to-do sheet.

TO DO TODAY

Date: October 10

Priority	Task	Complete
1	Study for History test	
2	Research Literature paper	X
1	Write Biology lab report	
3	Call Peter about book fair	X
2	Pick up test blue book	X
3	Meet with Ms. Keller about speech due next week	X
1	Review notes from English lecture	X

Leading Time Wasters

Have you every tried to study, sleep, watch TV, or talk with a friend and were constantly interrupted? No doubt, whether you live at home or in the dorm, you have distractions that keep you from completing tasks that need to be finished or things that you really want to do. Time wasters are a *big* problem in a time-management system. Recognizing distractions and attempting to ignore them is a major hurdle in the time-management game. Some of the leading time wasters are:

TIME WASTERS

- Friends who call or show up unexpectedly
- Television
- The telephone
- Trying to get so "organized" that you never get anything accomplished
- Being distracted by equipment you are using (computer: playing computer games instead of working on a program, etc.)

- The weather
- A messy house or dorm
- A hobby
- Procrastination

What are some time wasters that you have encountered? _____

_____

_____

What are some of the ways you can eliminate these time wasters? _____

_____

_____

Procrastination: The Enemy of the Student

"I'll do that in a little while;" how many times have you said this? Procrastination, or the art of putting off until tomorrow what you could do today can kill the best study plan. It is easy to procrastinate. Even the best of time managers have to fight this "enemy" every day. The good news is that *you* are in control. You choose when to complete or not complete assignments, and then, ultimately, you pay the consequences if you have procrastinated. The best way to fight procrastination is to jump right in—at least make an attempt to get started. You might want to break your study time up into fifteen-minute segments at first. Tell yourself, "If I finish fifteen minutes of productive studying, I will treat myself with a five-minute break." There are times when fifteen minutes might be all of the time you have. Try to begin learning to use this time effectively and efficiently. Later on, as you get more "into" your subject, you may want to increase the time to thirty minutes with a five-minute break. Be sure to give yourself a break—you have earned it!

Another way to avoid procrastination, and to deal effectively with trying to study when children are around, is to have group study time set aside for every student in the house. Everyone may want to sit down at the dinner table and begin to tackle the day's assignments. If you begin this at the beginning of the academic year, it will become a matter of routine—one that will take a priority in your home.

It Is All About Priorities!

By developing a priority system (a system that lets you know what is most important, next most important, and least important) of tasks that need to be accomplished, you create a much more efficient use of your time. One way to use your time more efficiently is to set up a system for prioritizing tasks that need to be accomplished. A simple list, on which you can assign a number or letter to let you know what is most important, next most important, and least important could be helpful. If you are a more visual learner, and need a different system, separate file folders labeled A, B, and C can be used. (This system is closely related to the to-do list discussed earlier in this chapter.) You can then prioritize your work and place it into the appropriate folder based on the following system:

A: Tasks that need to be completed immediately

B: Tasks that need to be completed within the next week

C: Tasks that can be completed at any later time

The A file or list would need your immediate attention. For example, any assignment that is due within the next few days needs to go to your A file or on your A list. Assignments that are more than a week away could go to your B file or on your B list. Naturally, you would need to review what is in your file system or list system every day; some B items will need to be given a higher priority as time goes on. The C folder or list is for information that either (1) may not have a specific due date or (2) can wait until there is free time. Occasionally, items in the C folder or C list will need to be reviewed to make sure that you have properly prioritized your work. There may even be items in the C folder or on the C list that no longer require action.

REMEMBER!!

This system may not work for everyone! At least give this system a chance. If you find that it does not work for you, then abandon this idea and try the to-do list system discussed earlier.

A variety of time-management systems that you might find useful are available in stores. Some of these systems work very much like the folder or list system. These systems *work* and could be quite helpful to you as a student. The important factor with one of these time-management systems is that the system can only work if it is used. If you spend a great deal of money to purchase an elaborate system and then do not even attempt to use it, you will not receive any of the benefits. Finding a system that is workable for you can greatly increase your chances of success. Successful people almost always have a time-management system that they have developed over a period of time. Talk to successful students and ask them which system they use. Sharing helpful tips on time management can help you as well as other students.

Roadways to Effective Time Management

TIME-MANAGEMENT TIPS

- Work on your hardest subjects first; save the easiest items for last.

- Organize your free time into usable chunks. Five minutes here or there is of little or no value.

- Make lists, prioritize the lists, and follow the lists!

- Revise your to-do list every morning. Items that were not completed one day should be completed the next.

- Find a place that allows you to study without interruption. Do not allow others to interrupt your work.

- Utilize a folder system.

- Purchase a commercially available time-management system.

Observations

Why do we study time management? Ultimately, the answer is to be able to have more free time to do the things we want to do. Quite simply, if we manage our time effectively, we can do what we want. Time is a constant resource for everyone. Every person has the same amount of time. How one chooses to spend time is a matter of priorities. Having a realistic perception of time enables you to judge the passage of time more effectively. Knowing where your time goes and being able to recognize system-imposed time and non-system-imposed time can allow you to make prioritizations about your free time. Time management is a learned skill, one that will enable you to be a more successful student.

As a Result of this Chapter, and in Preparing for My Journey, I Plan to . . .

CHAPTER 4

Sights, Sounds and Sensations
Information Processing and Learning Styles

CHAPTER 4

> He who has no inclination to learn more will be very apt to think he knows enough.
> *Powell*

Math!! How André hated that subject. It didn't matter how hard André studied, he couldn't understand. He could remember his parents, teachers, and friends getting on his case about studying. André did study! He had tutors! But, nothing seemed to work. He was discouraged and frustrated, and knew he was doomed to never make a grade better than a C (and that was on a *good* day.)

One day all that changed. It was André's Freshman year in high school. He never forgot that first day in Mr. Lane's class. Mr. Lane explained that math was about to become everyone's favorite subject. André thought Mr. Lane was crazy! He knew he could never change his opinion of math.

As time passed, to André's surprise, Mr. Lane was able to change André's attitude toward math. Mr. Lane first explained how important it was that we think positively, and to believe that we could master numbers. Sure, some students would have to work hard to be successful, but Mr. Lane explained that in order to be successful in math, students needed to see it, hear it, and touch it. For example, he told them to use their fingers when counting and to remove their shoes and use their toes if needed.

He was an excellent teacher. He did show the class how to see, hear, and touch math. For the first time in his life, André understood what he was doing. It was as if someone had unlocked a door that was keeping him from learning. André got an 88 out of 100 on his first test. He even managed to pass the class with an 82!

Perhaps André's fear of math sounds familiar to you. The story about André is quite common. Many students share these same fears, anxieties, and academic frustrations about math and other subjects. Fortunately, Mr. Lane was there to show this student how to master difficult material.

Students often give up and/or quit learning new material because they cannot understand it right away. What they do not realize is that they have not been processing information correctly. André's story is a perfect example of how learning involves seeing, hearing, and touching the information in order to understand it.

The intention of this chapter is to show you how to become a successful student by applying information-processing theory and learning-style theory when trying to master information. This chapter will teach you how to use a holistic approach when processing information, and all five senses when learning to achieve academic success. Being a student means accepting responsibility for learning the information presented to you. In a nutshell, when you understand how material is processed by your brain and how to use your preferred learning style, you, too, can overcome academic barriers.

If you complete the exercises, participate in class, read the additional assignments that may be issued by your instructor, and keep an open mind, at the end of this chapter, you will be able to do the following tasks:

- Define information-processing and learning-preference theories

- Identify your preferred learning style

- Create and use learning-style strategies to learn and recall information

- Use both a global and analytical approach to processing information

- Use mnemonic devices or memory tricks in order to store and recall information

Next you will find ten questions intended to cause you to think about how you learn and process information.

SELF-STUDY

1. I know the senses that are used when students are learning.   *1 2 3 4 5*

2. I know my preferred learning style.   *1 2 3 4 5*

3. I know how I process information.   *1 2 3 4 5*

4. I use a variety of senses when studying and learning.   *1 2 3 4 5*

5. I know how a visual learner processes information.   *1 2 3 4 5*

6. I know how an auditory learner learns.   *1 2 3 4 5*

7. I know how a kinesthetic learner learns.   *1 2 3 4 5*

8. I know the characteristics of a global thinker.   *1 2 3 4 5*

9. I use mnemonic devices.   *1 2 3 4 5*

10. I believe learning is fun.   *1 2 3 4 5*

5=Strongly Agree
4=Agree
3=Don't Know
2=Disagree
1=Strongly Disagree

TOTAL YOUR POINTS from these ten questions. How did you do? Do you feel good about your score? Use the following rating scale to determine how much you know about how to learn information.

0–10   Your understanding of how to learn is poor.

11–20 Your understanding of how to learn is below average.

21–30 Your understanding of how to learn is average.

31–40 Your understanding of how to learn is above average.

41–50 Your understanding of how to learn is excellent.

Information-Processing Theory

Learning and processing information are primarily functions of the brain. The human brain is divided into two halves, called hemispheres, that deal with information in different ways. The hemispheres are the left and right hemispheres. The brain functions best when both sides are able to work together, each complementing the other. The left hemisphere is the part of the brain that does the thinking and reasoning. It offers most of the characteristics associated with analytical thinking. The right hemisphere is the part of the brain that feels and acts. It gives us most of the characteristics associated with global thinking. The two styles of thinking are of equal importance (one balancing the other), with each contributing in its own way to learning and information processing.

Traditional school settings are designed to meet the needs of students who think analytically (students who find reading, writing, and math easy to learn). However, there are many students who fail to learn in school or experience difficulties understanding new information. Many of these students are global thinkers and need to use this strength to master the analytical skills.

When students use analytical and global thinking together (using the whole brain), learning becomes easier. As a student, it is your responsibility to realize what type of thinker you are (analytical or global) and how to use both styles of thinking at the same time.

It is important that you understand that you have strengths associated with both styles of processing. Everyone, however, has a dominant style. The following inventory will help you to identify the style of thinking that is dominant.

INFORMATION-PROCESSING INVENTORY

Directions: First, read through the statements. After you have read all the statements for both A and B traits, check the statements that are most like you. Please keep in mind that there are no right or wrong answers.

A Traits

_____ I am good at remembering faces.

_____ I remember information best when someone has shown me how to do it.

_____ I like expressing my feelings.

_____ I enjoy doing many things at once.

_____ I can sense how someone feels.

_____ I can create funny things to say or do.

_____ I like having fun when I am doing things.

_____ I like studying in groups.

_____ I am easily distracted.

_____ I am unorganized.

_____ I enjoy art or music or dance.

_____ I prefer essay tests.

_____ I like meeting new people.

_____ I make decisions with my heart.

_____ I like to answer questions by guessing.

_____ I don't pay attention to details.

_____ I learn best by seeing or doing.

_____ I have difficulty following directions.

_____ I use my hands when I talk.

_____ I lose track of time.

B Traits

_____ I am good at remembering names.

_____ I remember information best when I can read about it.

_____ I do not like expressing how I feel.

_____ I like to work on one thing at a time.

_____ I usually cannot tell how someone is feeling.

_____ I find it difficult to create funny things to say or do.

_____ I like to be serious when doing things.

_____ I prefer to study alone.

_____ I am not easily distracted.

_____ I am organized.

_____ I enjoy reading or math or science.

_____ I prefer multiple-choice tests.

_____ I make decisions with my head.

_____ I am uncomfortable meeting new people.

_____ I like to think through questions before answering them.

_____ I pay attention to details

_____ I learn best by hearing about things.

_____ I can follow directions.

_____ I rarely use my hands when I talk.

_____ I can keep track of time.

Now, count the number of checks you made for A and B and record the totals:

_____ Total A traits

_____ Total B traits

A traits are characteristics associated with *global thinking*.
B traits are characteristics associated with *analytical thinking*.

CHARACTERISTICS OF ANALYTICAL AND GLOBAL THINKERS

Analytical Thinkers

Concerned with details

Organized

Predictable

Auditory

Consecutive

Aware of time

Math (algebra)

Reading, spelling, writing

Practical

Logical

Focused

Global Thinkers

Concerned with the big picture

Unorganized

Spontaneous

Visual and kinesthetic

Random

Unaware of time

Geometry (shapes, etc.)

Music, art, drama, dance

Creative

Instinctive

Easily distracted

Most individuals spend about 70% of their time completing and participating in analytical activities and only about 30% of their time doing global activities. By learning how to develop both styles of processing or thinking, students can significantly improve their ability to learn.

Since everyone has a preference for one style of thinking or the other, the key to successful learning is to use both styles of thinking at the same time. For example, if you are unorganized and always forgetting assignments, then writing down assignments would be very helpful to you as a student. In addition, when taking notes, you might find it helpful to use colored pens and pencils. The color is helpful because it stimulates global processing while completing the analytical skill of taking notes. When learning vocabulary, you might use index cards. Flashing through the cards is a global activity that helps the analytical processing needed to develop vocabulary.

By learning to use both styles of thinking at the same time, it is easy to see that retaining and understanding becomes much easier. Albert Einstein and Pablo Picasso, along with many other scientists and artists, saw the value of using styles of thinking. These individuals had well-developed analytical and global thinking skills. The following information describes strategies for activating analytical and global processing.

ANALYTICAL PROCESSING OR THINKING

When learning, analytical thinkers prefer

- Bright light
- Quiet study environment
- Working on one activity at a time
- Studying alone
- Formal or traditional learning environment

GLOBAL PROCESSING OR THINKING

When learning, global thinkers prefer

- Short breaks
- Low lighting
- Eating/drinking while learning
- Music or sound in the background
- Informal or comfortable learning environment
- Working on many activities at one time
- Studying in groups

BRAIN TEASER

This activity does not measure your intelligence, your fluency with words, or your mathematical ability. It will, however, give you some indication of your mental flexibility and creativity. It will require that you draw from both styles of thinking in order to achieve success. Few people can solve more than half of the items, so don't get discouraged if you have trouble.

Example: 4 W on a C   4 Wheels on a Car

                 13 O C   Thirteen Original Colonies

1. SW and the 7 D _____
2. I H a D by M L K _____
3. 2 P's in a P _____

4. H D D (T M R U T C) _____
5. 3 S to a T _____
6. 100 P in a D _____
7. T No P L H _____
8. 4 Q in a G _____
9. I a S W A A _____
10. 50 S in T U _____

Learning Preference Theory

Many of you have undoubtedly wondered how information gets to your brain. This information travels along several very common avenues or pathways. When you are learning or processing information, you are in fact using one or more of your five basic senses (sight, touch, sound, smell, or taste) to gather information for your brain to process. Successful learning of new information occurs when you use as many of your senses as you can to transmit the new material to the brain.

Everyone has a preferred learning style or dominant sense that they use to learn information, especially information that may be difficult. For instance, have you ever asked someone to write something down, to repeat what they said, or even to let you try your hand at it in an effort to understand? If you've made these comments, chances are you were trying to get the information presented in such a way that you could best understand it.

Most students use a combination of senses to help guarantee that the brain will understand the material. If you are learning a new song, for instance, your sense of *hearing* is challenged more than the other senses. Sight may also play a part in the learning process since you can *see* the musical notes. In addition, by using a musical instrument to play the song, you would be using *touch* to learn the song. These examples reveal that you can use a combination of senses of hearing, seeing, and touching to experience a new song. In all likelihood, your chances of mastering the song will be increased if you involve several of your senses.

Another illustration of how you might combine your senses to learn about a subject might occur if you are studying a new type of flower. You may first examine it closely. Next, you may smell it's scent. You may also be able to taste the flower if it is edible, and finally you may even observe how it feels. Once again, you would be using several of your senses (sight, smell, taste, and touch) to identify the new flower.

If information is received through as many of the senses as possible, you were more likely to understand a new concept. Using the five senses (sight, smell, taste, touch, and sound), explain how you would teach the following items to someone who has never been exposed to that item before. Be creative and have fun.

Lesson 1: A vocabulary word: beautiful

Sight _____

Smell _____

Taste _____

Touch _____

Sound _____

Lesson 2: A math problem: 2 + 2 = 4

Sight _____

Smell _____

Taste _____

Touch _____

Sound _____

Lesson 3: To spell the word: success

Sight _____

Smell _____

Taste _____

Touch _____

Sound _____

Lesson 4: An object: a lemon

Sight _____

Smell _____

Taste _____

Touch _____

Sound _____

After completing the activity, answer the following questions:

1. Were you able to use all of the senses each time? Why or why not? _____
_____
_____
_____

2. Which senses were harder to use? Why do you think they were harder to use?
_____
_____
_____

3. Which senses do you feel students use when they are learning new information? Why? _____
_____
_____

How Do You Learn?

As you have discovered, effective learning involves a variety of our senses. We all learn differently, and some students must use specific senses in order to learn. Students generally use one or more of the following senses when learning a new skill: visual (sense of sight), auditory (sense of sound), and/or kinesthetic (sense of touch). Each student has a preferred style that they use regularly to achieve academic success. Which style do you think you use most often? Circle your preferred style:

Visual   **Auditory**   **Kinesthetic**

It is important that you know your preferred style and how to use the other styles to reach your academic potential. Knowing about other learning styles can also help when the material seems difficult to learn. The inventory that follows will identify your preferred learning style.

LEARNING PREFERENCE INVENTORY

Before completing this activity read each statement in each category. For each of the following categories, circle the appropriate number for each statement. Please keep in mind that there are no right or wrong answers.

1 = least like me

2 = sometimes like me

3 = most like me

"A" Learning Preference

1 2 3   In my spare time, I enjoy watching TV or reading a magazine.

1 2 3   When putting something together, I need to look at the drawing.

1 2 3   I like teachers who write on the board and use visual aids.

1 2 3   I need to see things in order to remember them.

1 2 3   When I solve a word problem in math, I draw pictures.

1 2 3   I need a map in order to find my way around.

1 2 3   I can tell how someone feels by the expression on his/her face.

1 2 3   At a meeting, I prefer to watch people.

"B" Learning Preference

1 2 3   In my spare time, I enjoy listening to music or talking on the phone.

1 2 3   When putting something together, I need for someone to explain how to do it.

1 2 3   I like teachers who lecture about course information.

1 2 3   I need to hear things to remember them.

1 2 3   When I solve math word problems, I need to talk them out.

1 2 3   When getting directions, I need to hear them.

1 2 3   I can tell how people feel by the sound of their voice.

1 2 3   At a meeting, I prefer to listen and talk to people.

"C" Learning Preferences

1 2 3   In my spare time, I enjoy physical activities (running, playing ball, etc.)

1 2 3   When putting something together, I need for someone to show me how to do it.

1 2 3   I like teachers who provide classroom activities and encourage student involvement.

1 2 3   I need to write things down in order to remember them.

1 2 3   When I solve word problems in math, I prefer that someone show me what to do.

1 2 3   When getting directions, I need to write them down to remember them.

1 2 3   At a meeting, I prefer to take part in the conversation or activities.

_____ Total "A" learning preference

_____ Total "B" learning preference

_____ Total "C" learning preference

"A" learning preference is *visual*, the sense of sight.
"B" learning preference is *auditory*, the sense of sound.
"C" learning preference is *kinesthetic*, the sense of touch.

It is important to note that there are *no* right or wrong answers. We are all different, and we all learn differently. One style is not more important or better than the other, and you may see a little of yourself in all preferences. This inventory indicates the style you prefer when learning new material. The following information describes the three types of learners and strategies for using that style.

VISUAL LEARNERS

Visual learners learn information through their sense of sight. They need to see in order to understand and remember. This learning style is the most common. The following activities help to develop visual strengths:

- Reading or studying the written word, pictures, or charts

- Taking notes (especially in color)
- Drawing pictures or diagrams of information
- Visualizing information in your mind

AUDITORY LEARNERS

Auditory learners learn information through their sense of sound. They need to hear something to learn and remember it. Approximately 80% of the material presented in high school and college is taught in this way. Therefore, it is extremely important that you develop this learning style in order to achieve academic success. The following activities help to develop auditory skills:

- Being silent and listening
- Focusing on what your teachers are saying
- Making audiotapes of class lectures and discussions
- Talking to yourself or others about the information
- Studying in a group

KINESTHETIC LEARNERS

Kinesthetic learners learn best through their sense of touch. Students who learn in this way must physically experience the information to understand and remember it. The following activities help to develop the kinesthetic sense:

- Acting out the information (role playing)
- Using your hands to experience something
- Making models, charts, diagrams, and so forth
- Taking notes
- Adding movement when studying (such as walking, tapping a finger, or rocking in a chair)
- Chewing gum
- Studying in a group

Learning new information can sometimes be difficult. It may sometimes even be easy. Regardless of its difficulty level, to successfully master new material students should involve as many of their senses as possible. Learning new information can be easy and fun with the help of your senses.

Using Mnemonic Devices

Our ability to retrieve information from our memory is a function of how well it was learned in the first place.

Josh R. Gerow

People forget about 98% of what they learn. This is an alarming statistic, especially when you consider the enormous amount of time and effort that many of you put into studying. Understanding human memory and applying memory techniques can help guarantee that you will be able to recall the information you have studied for an exam. According to psychologists, there are three types of human memory:

Sensory memory

Working memory

Long-term memory

Sensory memory stores information gathered from your five senses. This memory is usually temporary unless it is important to you. Working memory is the information gathered from your senses that you feel is important. You can only store a limited amount of information in your working memory. If you want to ensure that you remember this information, then you must store it in your long-term memory. Long-term memory is where information is stored permanently. How you organize and remember information is extremely important.

In many ways, your brain is like a room with file cabinets along its walls. On the floor in the middle of the room is a huge pile of papers. Each sheet of paper contains a separate and distinct piece of information. This pile of papers is your working memory. As the pile gets larger and larger, pieces of information get covered up and forgotten. The only way to move this pile of working memory into long-term memory (where it will not be forgotten) is to organize it and to place it into one of the file cabinets along the wall. You can, for example, put equations into a folder in the math file cabinet. (This folder in the math file cabinet may hold equations that solve certain types of math problems). You can also put a word's definition into a folder in the language file cabinet.

One way to organize this information is to use mnemonic devices or memory tricks. Mnemonic devices help you to store information in your long-term memory by associating that information with information you already know (putting it into a folder).

There are five basic types of mnemonic devices:

1. **Jingles/rap:** You can create jingles and rhymes to remember information. *Example:* Columbus sailed the ocean blue in 1492.

2. **Associations:** Create associations by putting words, ideas, and symbols together to remember information. *Example:* Light bulb = an idea; tomahawk = Atlanta Braves.

3. **Sentences:** Create a sentence using the first letter in each word from a list of information that you want to remember. *Example:* To remember the order of operations in math, use "Please excuse my dear Aunt Sally." This stands for *p*arentheses, *e*xponents, *m*ultiply, *d*ivide, *a*dd and *s*ubtract.

4. **Words:** Create a word to represent the information you need to remember. *Example:* To remember the colors in the spectrum, use the name Roy G. Biv (this stands for *r*ed, *o*range, *y*ellow, *g*reen, *b*lue, *i*ndigo, and *v*iolet).

5. **Visualize:** Create a picture in your mind of what you want to remember. *Example:* Italy looks like a boot on a map.

Create a mnemonic for the following concepts:

1. Parts of speech (nouns, pronouns, verbs, adverbs, adjectives, prepositions, conjunctions, and interjections) _____

_____

_____

_____

2. The five great lakes (Michigan, Erie, Superior, Huron, Ontario) _____

_____

_____

_____

_____

3. The first five Presidents of the United States (Washington, Adams, Jefferson, Madison, and Monroe) _____

_____

_____

_____

_____

4. The seven continents (North America, South America, Europe, Asia, Africa, Antarctica, and Australia) _____
_____
_____
_____

5. The nine planets (Mercury, Venus, Earth, Mars, Jupiter, Saturn, Uranus, Neptune, and Pluto) _____
_____
_____
_____

ROADWAYS TO LEARNING AND PROCESSING INFORMATION

- **Become actively involved when studying, reading, and taking notes. Ask yourself questions to keep yourself focused. Draw visual diagrams; study with friends.**

- **Get organized! Develop a note-taking system, record assignments, and keep an organized notebook.**

- **Your study environment should be quiet and free of distractions (phone, friends, etc.).**

- **Use colored pens and pencils when taking notes and studying.**

- **Create movement when studying. Walk, march, tap a finger, and so on.**

- **Use mnemonics or memory tricks to store and retrieve information.**

- **Get involved! Use both styles of thinking and as many senses as possible when learning.**

Observations

Your academic success is entirely your responsibility. Your instructors might not teach in the way that is best for you. There also may be academic subjects that you find difficult. Regardless, you are ultimately responsible for mastering the information. Do not let your academic subjects get the better of you.

Learn to take charge! Remember to learn and to study new information using both styles of thinking. In addition, use as many senses as possible when learning and studying. Since success is within your reach, you must grasp it by applying the techniques mentioned in this chapter. You can truly achieve academic success. The road is yours to travel.

As a Result of this Chapter, and in Preparing for My Journey, I Plan to . . .

CHAPTER 5

Scanning the Radio
The Powerful Art of Listening

CHAPTER 5

It is the province of knowledge to speak, and it is the privilege of wisdom to listen.
Unknown

Freshman year! Day one! First class! The History of Western Civilization! Instructor, Miss Wilkerson!!! "Your life will never be the same after you leave here," were her first words. She meant every one of them. Miss Wilkerson had been an award-winning basketball coach for almost twenty years and had retired to teach college history. She was tough in class, tough in notes, you'll learn more about history than you ever dreamed possible. If you come to me unprepared, you will not know if you are in Egypt, Mesopotamia, or pure hell!!! Class dismissed!"

With horror and fear running through our bodies, my friend and I left the class bewildered and exhausted. We had never seen anything like it before. She was a tornado—a 65-year-old tornado!

It is doubtful that you will complete your degree without running into a "Miss Wilkerson" from time to time. You may have already encountered her, or professors like her, who speak so rapidly that you have to have a sixth sense just to keep up the pace. The nation's campuses are filled with Miss Wilkersons. She was a fantastic teacher, but she moved through the material at the speed of sound. The students had to learn how to listen as quickly as she spoke, and keep up with her, or withdraw from the class.

How important do you feel listening skills are to your success as a student? A very important step in becoming a good student is knowing how to listen and evaluate the information that is heard. This chapter is intended to assist you in developing your listening skills and to become a better listener. In becoming a more active listener, you will be able to take better notes in class, participate more, and retain more information. Upon completion of this chapter, you will be able to

- Distinguish the difference between listening and hearing
- Explain the listening process of receiving, focusing, interpreting, and responding
- Define effective listening
- Recognize and eliminate the roadblocks to effective listening
- Identify active and passive listening characteristics
- Use the four-step process for "Getting Others to Listen to Me"
- Understand and use Roadways to Active Listening

Next you will find some statements to help you assess where you are as a listener at this moment. Take your time and evaluate each question carefully.

the hallway, tough in her office, tough in the parking lot, tough while giving notes, tough when reviewing for a test, and even tougher when test day arrived. She was tough!!!

Usually, on the first day of classes, the instructor would go over the syllabus, talk about the class, and let the students go. "Don't expect to leave here one second before *my* time is up," she said. "You paid for history and that is exactly what you are going to get." She reviewed the syllabus, spoke briefly about the class, and began to lecture on the Mesopotamian Civilization. The entire class scrambled for a notebook and pen. Most of us would have written on anything not to miss a word of what she was saying. For the next thirty-seven minutes, we listened—she talked. Our hands were hurting as we tried to write at the speed at which she lectured, wrote on the board, and used the overhead.

Shortly before our fifty-minute period was over, she closed her book and said the words that I remember verbatim eighteen years later. "You'd better get ready. Do not come to this class unprepared. Bring your notebook, textbook, five pencils or two pens with you daily. I shall not stop this class for you to sharpen or borrow an instrument.

"You will come to this class ready to *listen* to me. You will not talk to your friends during my class. If you stick with me, listen to me carefully, and take your

SELF-STUDY

1. I know how to listen with my whole body. *1 2 3 4 5*
2. I enjoy listening. *1 2 3 4 5*
3. I know how to listen for cues. *1 2 3 4 5*
4. I ask questions when listening. *1 2 3 4 5*
5. I know how to listen in different settings. *1 2 3 4 5*
6. I can identify the process of listening. *1 2 3 4 5*
7. I often stop listening when I don't agree. *1 2 3 4 5*
8. I stop listening if I don't like the speaker. *1 2 3 4 5*
9. I know the difference between active and passive listening. *1 2 3 4 5*
10. I know how to get others to listen to me. *1 2 3 4 5*

5=Strongly Agree
4=Agree
3=Don't Know
2=Disagree
1=Strongly Disagree

TOTAL YOUR POINTS from these ten questions. Refer to the following rating scale to determine where you stand in relation to your active listening skills.

0–10   *You have a great deal of difficulty focusing on the message and actively listening.*

11–20 *Your ability to focus and your listening skills are below average.*

21–30 *Your ability to focus and actively listen is average.*

31–40 *Your ability to focus and actively listen is above average*

41–50 *You have excellent listening skills. You are able to focus on the message and weed out distractions.*

Does your score match the way you feel about your listening skills? Why or why not? If your score indicates that your listening skills are less than average, relax; this chapter is included to assist you in increasing your listening skills.

To Be a Captain, You First Have to Be a Sailor

There are many connections and relationships that have to be made to survive in this world. You've already figured out many of them, or you wouldn't be in college. As the heading of this section states, to be a captain, you have to know how to be an

effective sailor. You may have even read the quote by the poet, Ralph Waldo Emerson, "The only way to have a good friend is to be one." The same connection can be made between listening and note taking. If you do not have the needed listening skills, it is very unlikely that you will be able to take useful notes in class.

Listening is one of the most important and useful skills we possess. To all animals, including humans, listening is a survival skill. For many animals, it is necessary to avoid predators and sustain life. For others, it is necessary for hunting and finding food. For humans, listening is necessary for the establishment of relationships, growth, survival, knowledge, entertainment, and even health. It is one of the most important and widely used tools humans possess. How much time per day do you think you spend in listening situations? Research suggests that we spend almost 70% of our waking time communicating (Adler, 1989). Fifty-three percent of that time is spent in listening situations. Effective listening skills can mean the difference between success or failure, A's or F's, relationships or loneliness.

For students, listening is a skill critical to success. Much of the information that you will receive over the next two to four years will be provided to you in the lecture format. Cultivating and improving your active listening skills will assist you in understanding the lecture, taking accurate notes, participating in class discussions, and communicating with your peers.

The Difference between Listening and Hearing

We usually do not think much about listening until a misunderstanding occurs or something goes wrong. You've probably been in a situation when someone misunderstood you or you misunderstood someone. These misunderstandings usually occur because we tend to view listening as an automatic response, when in actuality, listening is a *learned, voluntary* activity just as driving a car, painting a picture, or playing the piano is. Having ears does not make us good *listeners*. To make this assumption would be as illogical as believing that because we are given hands, we would be able to paint the Mona Lisa. True, we *may* be able to paint the Mona Lisa, but not without practice and guidance. Listening, too, takes practice, time, mistakes, guidance, and active participation before you can become an active listener.

Hearing is not learned. It is *automatic* and *involuntary*. As a matter of fact, if you are within the range of the sound that is made, you will probably hear it. This does not mean, however, that you were listening to it. Just because we heard the sound does not guarantee that we know what the sound was, or from where it came. To be actively listening, we would have to make a conscious effort to focus in on the sound and determine what the sound was.

Listening is a four-step process. It can be remembered by using the mnemonic, ROAR.

R—*Receiving* the information

O—*Organizing* the sounds heard and focusing on them

A—*Assigning* meaning

R—*Reacting*

The cycle can be shown as:

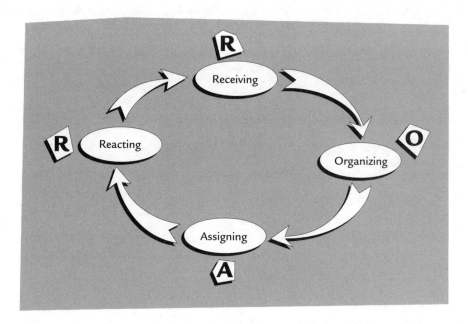

Receiving simply means that you were within the range of the sound that was made. It may have been a baby crying, a dish breaking, or a human voice speaking. Receiving the sound does not mean that you are listening.

To become an active listener, when *Receiving* the information, make an effort to

1. Tune out distractions other than the conversation at hand

2. Avoid interrupting the speaker

3. Pay close attention to nonverbal communication such as gestures, facial expressions, and movement

4. Focus not on what will be said next, but concentrate on what is being said at the moment

5. Listen for what is *not* said

Take a moment a determine what sounds you are receiving at this exact moment. List them. _____

_____

_____

Organizing and *Focusing* is when we choose to actively listen to the sound and pay attention to its origin, direction, and intention. Your mind begins to organize the information that was heard. You just did this in the exercise above.

Spend the next few moments talking with your partner in the class. Put your pen down and just listen carefully and actively; do not take notes on the conversation. Spend at least four to five minutes talking to your partner. Ask him/her about their goals, dreams, plans, major, and life's work. Now, in the space below, paraphrase what your partner said to you.

_____

_____

_____

_____

If you were actively listening, you would be able to write about his/her goals, major, dreams, and career. How did you do? Were you actively listening?

To become an active listener, when *Organizing* and focusing on the information, make an effort to

1. Sit up straight or stand near the person speaking so that you involve your entire body

2. Give the person eye contact, and listen with your eyes and ears

3. Try to create a visual picture of what is being said

Assignment is when we mentally assign a name or meaning to what we have been listening to. We may have to pay special attention to some sounds to assign them the correct name or meaning. Have you ever been sitting in your room and heard a crash? If so, you might have to have hear it again before you could name the sound of the crash as being dishes falling, books dropping, or static on the radio. Your brain is trying to make a relationship between what you just heard and what you have heard before. It is trying to associate one piece of information with another. When this is done, you will be able to identify the new sound by remembering the old sound.

To become an active listener, when *Assigning* meaning to information, make an effort to

1. Relate the information to something that you already know

2. Ask questions to ensure that there are no misunderstandings

3. Identify the main ideas of what is being said

4. Try to summarize the information into small "files" in your memory

5. Repeat the information to yourself (or out loud if appropriate)

When you are listening in class and taking notes, you will find information that is similar to or related to previous information heard. For instance, if you hear about *Oedipus Rex* in Theatre class, you might immediately relate it to the Oedipus complex in Psychology class. If you hear about Einstein in History, you will probably make the connection from Science. Active listening allows us to make associations, thus assisting us in creating learning patterns for long-term memory. Simply hearing the information will not allow you to make these relationships.

Listen carefully to the sounds made by your professor. He or she will ask you to close your eyes and listen actively. Try to identify them without asking for them to be repeated.

Sound 1 _____

Sound 2 _____

Sound 3 _____

Reacting is nothing more than our response to the sound that was heard. If we hear a crash, we may jump; if we hear a baby crying, we may pick it up; if we hear a voice, we may turn to see if we know the person speaking. Our reaction can also be a barrier to active listening. Have you ever tuned out or shut off someone because they were boring or because you did not agree with their point of view? If so, it is important to note that this is still a reaction to the information. It is impossible to have no reaction.

To become an active listener, when *Reacting* to information, make an effort to

1. Leave your emotions behind and not prejudge

2. Avoid overreacting

3. Avoid jumping to conclusions

4. Ask yourself, "How can this information help me?"

Practical Definitions of Listening

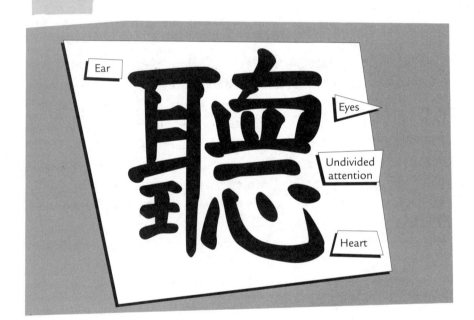

Perhaps the drawing of the Chinese verb "to listen" is the most comprehensive and practical definition that can be given. To the Chinese, listening involves many parts of the body: the ears, the eyes, the mind, and the heart. Do you make it a habit to listen with more than your ears? The Chinese view listening as a whole body experience. Western cultures seem to have lost the ability to effectively involve the whole body in the listening process. We tend to use only our ears, and sometimes we don't even use them.

The American Heritage Dictionary defines listening as: "To make an effort to hear something; to pay attention; to give heed." While this definition is standard, it does not offer us a great deal of concreteness or direction. Listening needs to be personalized and internalized. In order to understand listening as a whole body experience, we can define listening on three levels:

LISTENING WITH A PURPOSE

LISTENING OBJECTIVELY

LISTENING CONSTRUCTIVELY

Listening with a purpose suggests that we have to recognize the different types of listening situations in which we might be involved, such as class, worship, entertainment, and relationships. We do not listen the same way in every situation. When we go to a concert, we turn on our concert ears; we are listening for enjoyment and excitement. Unless we are musicians, we do not take a pen and pad with us to take notes on the music. When you go to class, you are listening to gain a deeper understanding of the materials presented. Have you ever listened to a friend who needed advice? If so, you were listening with "different ears" than you would in a classroom or an entertainment setting. This may sound a bit elementary, but unless you understand the difference in listening situations in which you are to be involved, you will find listening to be a more difficult adventure. Each situation demands that we know which type of listening will be required. This is called listening with a purpose.

List some different listening situations in which you will be involved this semester.

1. _____
2. _____
3. _____

How do they differ?

1. _____
2. _____
3. _____

Listening objectively means that we are listening with an open mind. Few gifts that you give yourself will be greater than knowing how to listen without bias and prejudice. This is perhaps the most difficult aspect of listening. Have you ever had someone cut you off in the middle of a conversation or sentence because they disagreed with you? Has anyone ever left the room when you were giving your opinion of a situation? If so, you have experienced people who do not know how to listen objectively and with an open mind.

Many times, we tend to shut out or ignore things with which we do not agree or information that is obscure and removed from our lives. Listening objectively requires us to listen with an open mind and then make our decisions. So often, we do the reverse; we make judgments and then try to listen. Have you ever done this?

List three situations in which you might be involved this semester that would require you to listen with an open mind.

1. _____
2. _____
3. _____

Why would you have to have objectivity in listening in each of these situations?

1. _____
2. _____
3. _____

Listening constructively suggests that we listen with the attitude, "How can this be helpful to my life or my education?" It simply asks us to evaluate the information being given and determine if it has meaning for our lives. Sound easy? Actually, it is more difficult than it sounds because, once again, we tend to shut out information that we do not see as immediately helpful or useful. To be constructive listeners, we need to know how to listen and store information for later dates.

John was a student who disliked math very much. He could never understand why, as a history major, he had to learn algebra. So, he would automatically tune out the math professor when she presented information that he did not see as necessary. From time to time we've all possibly felt this way about some piece of information or another. However, when we tune out because we cannot see, or refuse to see, the relationship to our lives, we are not constructively listening.

When was the last time you tuned out of a listening situation for any reason? Why?

_____
_____
_____
_____

Looking back, could you have benefited from the information or the source of the information had you not tuned out of the listening situation? Why or why not?

_____
_____
_____
_____

Obstacles to Listening

There are several major obstacles to becoming an effective listener. In order to begin building active listening skills, you first have to remove some barriers.

OBSTACLE ONE: PREJUDGING

Prejudging is one of the biggest obstacles to active listening. Prejudging means that you automatically shut out what is being said for several reasons. You may prejudge because of the content, or you may prejudge because of the person communicating. Prejudging can also evolve from environment, culture, social status, or attitude.

Willistine enrolled in a religion class at her college. The course was entitled "Faith, Doubt and Reason." Shortly after the class began, the instructor began asking questions and making statements that challenged what Willistine had believed all of her life. The instructor was trying to get the class to explore thoughts beyond what they held at that moment. After two weeks in the class, Willistine decided to drop the course because she did not want to hear the instructor's comments. Willistine was prejudging. She shut out what the instructor was saying because it went against what she believed. It is almost impossible to prejudge and then actively listen. The best situation is to listen with an open mind, and then make judgements.

■ **DO YOU PREJUDGE INFORMATION OR THE SOURCE?** Answer yes or no to the questions below.

1. I tune out when something is boring.   Yes   No

2. I tune out when I do not agree with the information.   Yes   No

3. I argue mentally with the speaker about information.   Yes   No

4. I do not listen to people that I do not like.   Yes   No

5. I make decisions about the information before I understand all of the implications or consequences.   Yes   No

If you answered yes to two or more of the questions, you tend to prejudge the listening situation.

■ **TIPS FOR OVERCOMING PREJUDGING:**

1. Listen for information that may be valuable to you as a student. Some material may not be pleasant to hear, but it may be useful to you later on.

2. Listen to the message, not the messenger. If you do not like the speaker, try to go beyond personality and listen to what is being said, not to the person saying it. This is a double-edged sword as well. You may like the speaker so much that you do not listen objectively to what is being said. You may accept the material or answers just because you like the person.

3. Try to remove cultural, racial, gender, social, and environmental barriers. Just because a person is different from you or holds a varying point of view does not make them wrong. If someone is just like you and you hold the same points of view, this does not make that person right. Sometimes we have to cross cultural and environmental barriers to learn new material and see with brighter eyes.

OBSTACLE TWO: TALKING

No one, not even the best listener in the world, can listen when he or she is talking. Take a moment the next time you are talking with a friend and try it. Speak to them while they are speaking, and see if you know what they said. In order to become an effective listener, we must learn the power of silence. Silence gives us the opportunity to do several things: think, listen, and consider. By being silent, we allow ourselves to think about what is being said before we are required to respond. This small amount of time can be invaluable to effective listeners. Silence also allows us to listen. The physical impossibility of trying to both listen and talk is taxing and always unsuccessful. Silence also allows us the opportunity to consider what others are saying. It gives us time for reflection.

■ ARE YOU A TALKER RATHER THAN A LISTENER? Answer yes or no to the questions below.

1. I often interrupt the speaker so that I can say what I want.   Yes   No

2. I am thinking of my next statement while others are talking.   Yes   No

3. My mind wanders when others talk.   Yes   No

4. I answer my own questions.   Yes   No

5. I answer questions that are asked of *other* people.   Yes   No

If you answered yes to two or more of the questions, you tend to talk too much in the listening situation.

■ TIPS FOR OVERCOMING THE URGE TO TALK TOO MUCH:

1. Force yourself to be silent at parties, family gatherings, and friendly get-togethers. We're not saying be unsociable, but force yourself to be silent for ten minutes. You'll be surprised at what you *hear*. You may also be surprised how hard it is to do this. Test yourself.

2. Ask questions and then allow the other person to answer the question. Many times, we ask questions and either answer them ourselves or cheat the other person out of a response. Force yourself to wait until the person has formulated a response. By asking questions and waiting for an answer, we force ourselves to listen. A great deal can be learned by questioning.

OBSTACLE THREE: BRINGING YOUR EMOTIONS TO THE TABLE

A barrier to active listening is bringing your emotions to the listening situation. Our worries, problems, fears, and anger can prevent us from listening to the greatest advantage. Have you ever sat in a lecture, and before you knew what was happening, your mind was a million miles away because you were angry or worried about something? If so, you have experienced obstacle three—bringing your emotions to the table.

■ DO YOU BRING YOUR EMOTIONS TO THE LISTENING SITUATION? Answer yes or no to the questions below.

1. I get angry before I hear the whole story.   Yes   No

2. I look for underlying or hidden messages in the information.   Yes   No

3. Sometimes, I begin listening on a negative note.   Yes   No

4. I base my opinions on information others are saying or doing.   Yes   No

5. I readily accept information as correct from people whom I like or respect.   Yes   No

If you answered yes to two or more of the questions, you tend to bring your emotions to the listening situation.

■ TIPS FOR OVERCOMING EMOTIONS:

1. Know how you feel before you begin the listening experience. Take stock of your emotions and feelings before you enter the situation.

2. Focus on the message and determine how you can use the information.

3. Try to create a positive image about the message you are about to hear.

ACTIVE AND PASSIVE LISTENING CHARACTERISTICS

Active Listeners	Passive Listeners
Lean forward and sit up straight	Slouch and lean back in chairs
Give the speaker eye contact	Look around the room
Listen for what is not said	Hear scattered information
Are patient	Get frustrated easily
Leave emotions outside	Get angry at the speaker
Avoid jumping to conclusions	Make immediate assumptions
Ask questions	Speed the speaker along
Focus on the topic	Daydream
Have an open mind	Prejudge the speaker
React to ideas	React to the person speaking

Do not argue mentally	Create mental arguments
Empathize	Criticize
Tune out distractions	Are distracted easily

Listening is hard work. It is a voluntary, learned skill that few people ever truly master. Active listeners seek to improve their skills by constantly involving themselves in the communication process.

How Do I Get Others to Listen to Me?

As a college student, an employee, leader, spouse, or caregiver, there will be times when you want people to listen to your views and opinions. There will be times when you want to speak out at a club meeting, a civic group meeting, or the PTA and you want people to hear what you are saying. Here are several "roadways" that you can use as a student to help other people listen to you.

Repetition: Make an effort to state your main ideas or points more than one time during your conversation. We need to hear things as many as fourteen times to have them placed in our long-term memory. Repetition helps.

Movement: When you are speaking, use some degree of movement with your body, such as gestures

THE POWERFUL ART OF LISTENING

and facial expressions. If you are standing in front of a group of people, you might want to move from one side of the room to the other. However, it is important to remember *not* to pace needlessly.

Energy: When you are speaking and trying to get others to listen to you, be energetic and lively with your words. It is hard to listen to someone who speaks in the same tone all the time. Be excited about what you are saying and people will listen to you more easily. This is perhaps the single most important way to get people to listen to your views.

Creativity: This simply means that you need to have something to say when you are speaking, and you need to say it in a way that is creative, fresh, and new. You know how hard it is to listen to people who never say a thing. They talk all the time, but seldom say anything important. When you speak, make sure that you are making a contribution to the conversation.

Listening for Key Words, Phrases, and Hints

Learning how to listen for key words, phrases, and hints can assist you in becoming an active listener and a more effective note taker. For example, the English professor says, "There are ten basic elements to writing poetry;" you should jot down the number 10 at a heading labeled "Poetry," or number your page 1 through 10, leaving space for taking the actual notes. If the professor completes the lecture and you only have six elements to writing poetry, you know that you have missed a part of the lecture. At this point, you should ask questions.

Some key phrases and words that may assist you in becoming an active listener are

in addition	another way to	above all
most importantly	such as	specifically

you'll see this again	therefore	finally
for example	to illustrate	as stated earlier
in contrast	in comparison	nevertheless
characteristics	the main issue is	moreover
due to	as a result of	because
on the other hand		

Knowing how to pick up on professors' transition words will help you filter out information that is less important, thus listening more carefully to what is most important. It is also very helpful to know when the information is important, and you should be listening with careful attention when the professor:

Writes something on the board

Uses an overhead

Draws on a flipchart

Uses computer-aided graphics

Speaks in a louder tone or changes vocal patterns

Uses gestures more than usual

THE TOP TEN REASONS FOR ACTIVELY LISTENING

Once you have learned how to listen actively, there are several key benefits that will help you as a student, as an employee, and as a citizen.

1. You are exposed to more information and knowledge about the world, your peers, and yourself.

2. You can help others because you have listened to their problems, and fears. You can have a greater sense of empathy.

3. You can avoid more problems at school or work than people who do not listen.

4. You will be able to participate in life more fully because you will have a keener sense of what is going on in the world around you.

5. You will grow to have more friends and healthy relationships because people are drawn to people to whom they can talk and feel are giving them a sincere ear.

6. You will be able to ask more questions and gain deeper understandings about subjects that interest you or ideas you wish to explore.

7. You will be a more effective leader. People follow people whom they feel really listen to their ideas and give their views a chance.

8. You will be able to understand more about different cultures from around the world.

9. You will be able to make more logical decisions regarding pressing and difficult issues in your life and studies.

10. You will feel better about yourself because you will know in your heart and mind that you gave the situation the best that you could.

Test Your Listening Skills

On the following pages is a series of activities that will test your active listening skills. You will be assisted by your professor. The activities found in this section test a variety of listening situations. You will need to use several types of listening skills to actively participate.

Activity #1
Circles and Lines

Using the diagram, respond to the directions given by your instructor.

THE POWERFUL ART OF LISTENING 121

Activity #2
Cabbie

Close your book, listen to the instructor's story, and then follow the instructor's directions.

_____ 1. A thief approached the cabdriver at a traffic light.

_____ 2. The thief demanded money.

_____ 3. The thief was a man.

_____ 4. The cabdriver's window was down all the way when the thief approached the cab.

_____ 5. The cabdriver gave the thief the money.

_____ 6. Someone sped away with the money.

_____ 7. The money was on the dash of the cab.

_____ 8. The amount of money was never mentioned.

_____ 9. The story mentions only two people: the cabdriver and the thief.

_____ 10. The following statements are true:
Someone demanded money; the money was snatched up; a person sped away.

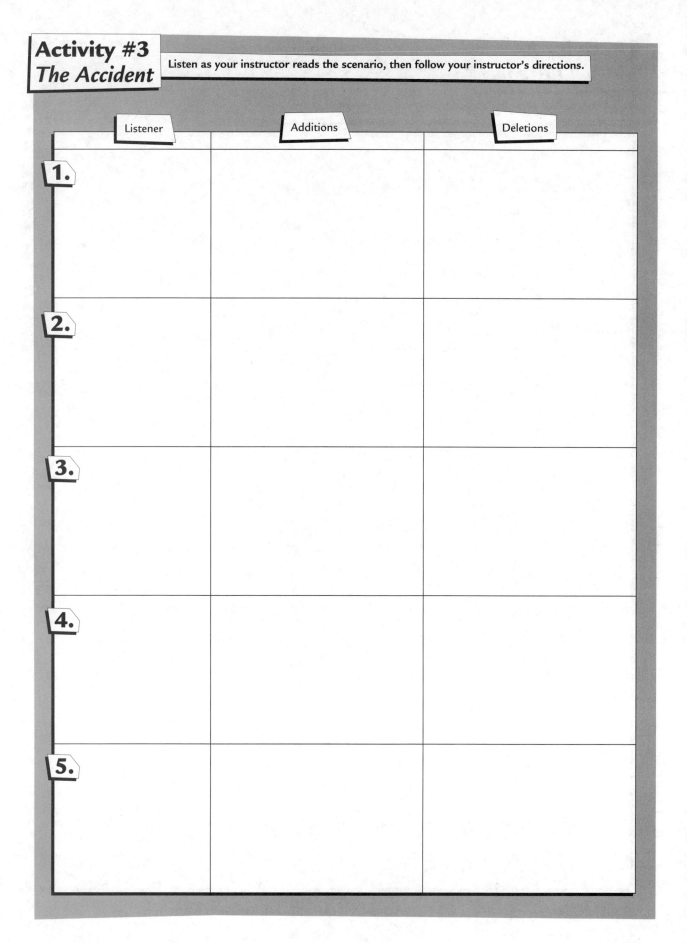

Activity #4
Visual Listening

Listen to your peers and draw the design that they verbally create.

Activity #5
Whispers

Write down what the person next to you whispers in your ear.

_____
_____
_____
_____
_____
_____
_____
_____
_____

Activity #6
I Can Name That Tune

After listening, answer the questions your instructor asks.

1. _____
2. _____
3. _____
4. _____
5. _____

Roadways to Active Listening

- Make the decision to listen. Listening is *voluntary*.
- Approach listening with an open mind.
- Leave your emotions at the door.
- Focus on the material at hand and how it can help you.
- Listen for key works and phrases.
- Listen for *how* something is said.
- Listen for what is *not* said.
- Stop talking.
- Eliminate as many distractions as possible.
- Listen for major ideas and details.
- Take notes; this makes you actively involved in listening.
- Paraphrase the speaker's words.
- Relate the information to something you already know.
- Encourage the speaker with your body language and facial expressions.
- Don't give up too soon; listen to the whole story.
- Avoid jumping to conclusions.

Observations

Listening to others and getting others to listen to us is hard, constant work. It takes a great deal of practice and time to master the skill of active listening and effective communication. Listening is a voluntary, learned skill that few master. Effective listeners always seek to improve their skills by actively involving themselves in the total communication process. To be an excellent note taker, your listening skills will have to be sharp and focused. Perhaps the most exciting thing about having superior listening skills is that you can learn new and exciting things, experience new information, and grow as a successful student and citizen.

As a Result of this Chapter, and in Preparing for My Journey, I Plan to . . .

CHAPTER 6

Charting Your Journey
The Process of Note Taking

CHAPTER 6

William loved to play pool. Pool was his passion, his hobby, his job, and his first love. Few things ever got in the way of William's pool game. On more than one occasion, William would cut class to go to the pool hall with his buddies from the dorm. "I'll just get the notes from Wanda," he said. "She's always there."

The pen is the tongue of the mind.

Unknown

When class met on Monday morning, William asked Wanda for her notes. She explained to him that her handwriting was not very good and that she took notes in her own shorthand. "Oh, that's all right," William said. "I'll be able to get what I need from them." Wanda agreed to make a copy of her notes for William and bring them to him on Wednesday.

Wanda kept her promise and brought a copy of her notes. William put them into his backpack just before class began. The notes stayed in his backpack until the night before the mid-term exam. He had not taken them out to look at them or to ask Wanda any questions about the notes. When he unfolded the notes and smoothed out the wrinkled pages, he was shocked at what he found. The notes read:

Psy started as a sci. disc. from Phi and Physio. Wihelm Wundt/GERM and Will James/US=fndrs. in lt. 19th cent. APA est. by Stanely Hall in US. 5 mjr Pers in PSY=

> *Biopsy. Per*
> *Psychodym. Per*
> *Humanistic. Per*
> *Cog. Per.*
> *Beh. Per.*

Psy wk in 2 mjr. areas 1. Acad. 2. Practicing

Needless to say, William was in much trouble. He could not understand Wendy's shorthand and had not bothered to ask her to translate her notes. To add insult to injury, William had lost his book a few weeks earlier. After trying to make sense of Wendy's notes, he gave up and went to the pool hall to relax and have fun before the test. William failed his mid-term.

We've all missed a few classes from time to time, haven't we? There are very few students who have not missed a class for one reason or another. There are two important reasons for attending every class meeting: first, if you are not there, you will not get the information presented; second, even if you get class notes from someone in the class, there is no substitute for your own notes. William had several problems, including setting priorities, but one of his biggest problems was that he was not in class to take his own notes. His other problem was that he did not bother to review the notes with Wendy and seek her understanding.

This chapter will deal with note taking and developing a system of note taking that works for you. At the end of this chapter, you will be able to

- Identify key phrases and words for effective note taking
- Understand why note taking is essential to successful students
- Use the L-STAR system
- Develop and use a personalized shorthand note-taking system
- Use the Outline technique
- Use the Mapping (or webbing) technique
- Use the Cornell (Split-T or Modified) technique
- Put into practice Roadways to Effective Note Taking

SELF-STUDY

5=Strongly Agree
4=Agree
3=Don't Know
2=Disagree
1=Strongly Disagree

1. I am an excellent note taker.
   1 2 3 4 5
2. I am a good listener.
   1 2 3 4 5
3. I have a personal note-taking system.
   1 2 3 4 5
4. I use abbreviations when taking notes.
   1 2 3 4 5
5. I use symbols when taking notes.   1 2 3 4 5
6. I pre-read each chapter before class. 1 2 3 4 5
7. I ask questions in class.
   1 2 3 4 5
8. I know how to listen for clues.   1 2 3 4 5
9. I re-write my notes after each class.
   1 2 3 4 5
10. I re-read my notes before each class.
    1 2 3 4 5

TOTAL YOUR POINTS from these ten questions. Refer to the following rating scale to determine where you stand in relation to note taking.

0–10 *You do not have a personalized system for note taking, and you probably do not take accurate notes.*

11–20 *You have some degree of note-taking skills, but you need to refine your skills by listening, using symbols, and abbreviations.*

21–30 *You are an average note taker. You pay some attention to style and content, and you probably read over your notes occasionally.*

31–40 *Your note-taking skills are above average. You probably read your notes weekly, correct any mistakes, and make additional notes in the margins.*

41–50 *Your note-taking skills are probably excellent. You re-write your notes, know how to use symbols and abbreviations, listen well, and probably have a personalized system of note taking.*

Does your score reflect how you truly feel about your note-taking skills? Why or why not? If you are disappointed in your score, relax; this chapter will help you become a more effective note taker by showing you a variety of note-taking systems.

Why Take Notes?

Is note taking really important, you might ask? Actually, knowing how to take useful, accurate notes can dramatically improve your life as a student. If you are an effective listener and note taker, you have two of the most valuable skills any student could ever use. It is important to take notes for several reasons:

1. You become an active part of the listening process.

2. It creates a history of your course content.

3. You have written criteria to follow when studying.

4. It creates a visual aid of your material.

As mentioned previously, listening is a learned skill, and so is note taking. Simply writing information down does not constitute note taking. There are note-taking systems and helpful clues that enable students to become more effective note takers. This chapter will discuss, review, and analyze these systems and methods and help you determine which works best for you. Just because your friend uses the outlining method does not make it right for you. If you are a visual learner, you may need to consider the mapping system. A note-taking system is personal and individualized. You will discover the best style for you as we move through this section of the chapter.

Do I Need to Write That Down?

College professors hear this question daily: "Do we need to write this down?" If it were up to most professors, they would have students write down the majority of what is said in class, but logically, they know this is impossible. Therefore, students who are effective listeners and note takers have figured out how to actively listen and distinguish the most important material covered. As discussed in the chapter on listening, they know how to listen for key words and phrases. To recap from the chapter on listening, some of the most important key phrases professors may use are:

in addition	another way to	you'll see this again
such as	most importantly	above all
finally	therefore	specifically
for example	to illustrate	as stated earlier
in contrast	in comparison	the main issue is
characteristics	due to	as a result of
because	on the other hand	nevertheless

Generally, when these phrases are used, you can be assured that the professor is making a major point and you need to listen carefully and write it down. Usually, if material is presented on an overhead, chalkboard, slickboard, or other media, you will need to take notes.

Preparing to Take Notes

In order to become an effective note taker, some preparations need to be made. An artist must have materials such as a brush, pallet, canvas, paints, and oils in order to create a painting. You must have certain materials and make detailed preparations for note taking.

Roadways of Effective Note Taking

ATTEND CLASS

This may sound completely elementary and out of place, but you will be surprised at how many college students feel that they do not need to go to class. "Oh, I'll just get the notes from Wanda," like William said in the opening story. The only trouble with getting the notes from Wanda is that they are *Wanda's notes.* You may be able to copy her words, but you may very well miss the meaning behind them. If Wanda has developed her own note-taking style, you may not be able to read many of her notes. She many have written something like this:

G/Oke lvd in C/SC for 1yr ely 20c.

Can you decode Wanda's notes? How would you ever know that these notes would translate to mean: "Georgia O'Keeffe lived in Columbia, South Carolina, for one year in the early part of the twentieth century"? In order to be an effective note taker, class attendance is very important. There is no substitute for it.

COME TO CLASS PREPARED

Do you read your assignments nightly? College professors are constantly amazed at the number of students who come to class and then decide that they needed to have read the homework materials. Reading your text, handouts, and workbooks or listening to tapes among the most effective ways to become a better note taker. It is always easier to write and take notes when you have a preliminary understanding of what is being said. Few student functions are more difficult than trying to take notes on material that you have never heard before. Preparing to take notes involves doing your homework and coming to class ready to listen.

Coming to class prepared also means that you have brought the proper materials to take notes. This means that you have your textbook or lab manual, at least two pens, enough *sharpened* pencils to make it through the lecture, a notebook, and a highlighter. Some students may also bring a tape recorder. If you choose to use a recorder, always get permission from the instructor before recording and don't depend solely on the recorder.

BRING YOUR TEXT TO CLASS

Many students do not feel as if they need to bring their text to class if they have read the homework. You will find that many professors will refer repeatedly to the text while lecturing. Always bring your text to class with you. This will assist you in your note-taking endeavors, especially if the professor asks you to highlight, underline, or refer to the text in class. Following the professor in the text as she lectures may also help you in organizing your notes.

ASK QUESTIONS AND PARTICIPATE IN CLASS!!

One of the most critical actions a student can perform in class is asking questions and actively participating in the class discussion. If you do not understand a concept or theory, it is imperative that you ask questions. It is not wise to just leave class without understanding what has happened. Many professors use student questions as a way of teaching and reviewing materials. Your questioning and participation will definitely help you, but it could also help others who do not understand. Asking questions moves you from a passive learner to an *active* learner.

Now, We're Ready to Begin the Building Process

At this point, you have been exposed to several thoughts about note taking. First, you know that you need to cultivate and build your active listening skills; second, you will need to overcome the obstacles to effective listening such as prejudging, talking during the discussion, and bringing emotions to the table; third, you will need to be familiar with key phrases used by professors; fourth, you need to understand the importance of note taking; fifth, you should prepare yourself to take effective notes; and finally, you now know that scanning, reading, and using your texts helps you understand the materials to be discussed.

The L-STAR System

One of the most effective ways to take notes begins with learning the L-STAR system. L-STAR stands for

L—*Listening*

S—*Setting it down*

T—*Translating*

A—*Analyzing*

R—*Remembering*

This five-step program allows you to compile complete, accurate, and visual notes for future reference. By using this system, you will greatly improve your ability to take accurate notes, participate in class, help other students, study more effectively, and perform well on your exams and quizzes.

L—LISTENING

As mentioned in the listening chapter, one of the best ways to become an effective note taker is to become an active listener. It is also important to sit near the front of the room so that you will be able to hear the professor and see the board and/or overheads. The best place to sit is in a place where you will be able to see the professor's facial expressions and mouth. If you see that the professor's face has become animated or expressive, you can bet that this information is important. Write it down. If you sit in the back of the room, you may not be able to hear or see certain expressions.

S—SETTING IT DOWN

The actual writing of notes can be a difficult task. Some professors are very organized in their delivery of information; others are not. Your listening skills, once again, are going to play an important role in determining what needs to be written down. In most cases, you will not have time to take notes verbatim. You will have to be more selective about the information you choose to set down. One of the best ways to keep up with the information being presented is to develop a shorthand system of your own. Many of the symbols will be universal, but you may use some symbols, pictures, and markings that are uniquely your own. Some of the more common symbols are

w/	with	w/o	without
=	equal	≠	does not equal
<	less than	>	greater than
%	percentage	#	number
@	at or about	$	money
&	and	^	increase

+	plus or addition	-	subtract
*	important	etc	and so on
eg	for example	(vs)	against
esp	especially	"	quote
?	question	...	and so on

These symbols can save you valuable time when taking notes. You may wish to memorize them, because you will use them frequently. As you become more adept at note taking, you will quickly learn how to abbreviate words, phrases, and names.

Using the symbols provided and your own shorthand system, practice reducing the following statements. Be sure that you do not reduce them to the extent that you will not be able to understand them at a later date.

1. It is important to remember that the greater the percentage of money invested does not necessarily equal greater profits.

Reduce: _____
_____
_____

2. She was quoted as saying, "Money equals success." Without exception, the audience disagreed with her logic.

Reduce: _____
_____
_____

3. He found a greater number of books at the new store than he thought. For example, there were over 1000 dictionaries available; a far greater number than at any other store.

Reduce: _____
_____
_____

4. The increase in scholarship money has allowed a greater number of students to attend college.

Reduce: _____
_____
_____

T—TRANSLATING

One of the most valuable things that you can do as a student is to translate your notes immediately after each class. This can save you hours of work when you begin to prepare for exams. Many students feel that this step is not important and leave it out. Don't. Many times, students take notes so quickly that they make mistakes or use abbreviations that they may not remember later.

After each class, go to the library or some quiet place and review your notes. It may not be possible to do this immediately after class, but before the day ends, you should have rewritten and translated your classroom notes. This will give you the opportunity to put the notes in your own words *and* incorporate your text notes into your classroom notes. You will also have a chance to correct spelling, reword key phrases, spell out your abbreviations, and prepare questions for the next class. Sounds like a lot of work, doesn't it? Well, it is a great deal of work, but if you try this technique for one week, you should see a vast improvement in your grades and understanding of material.

Translating your notes helps you to make connections between previous material discussed, your own personal experiences and readings, and new material presented. Translating helps in recalling and applying new information. Few things are more difficult than trying to reconstruct your notes the night before a test, especially when the notes may have been taken several weeks ago. Translating your notes daily will be a precious gift to yourself when exam time comes.

A—ANALYZING

This step happens when you are translating your notes from class. When you analyze your notes, you are asking yourself two basic questions:

1. What does this mean?

2. Why is it important?

If you can answer these two questions about your material, you have almost mastered the information. It is true that some instructors want you to "spit" back the same information you were given; most professors, however, will ask you for a more detailed understanding and application of the material. When you are translating your notes, begin to answer the two questions by using your notes, textbook, supplemental materials, and information gathered from outside research. Again, this is not simple or easy, but it is important to test yourself to see if you understand the information. It is important to note that many lectures are built on past lectures. If you do not understand what happened in class on September 17, you may not be able to understand what happens on September 19. Analyzing your notes while translating will give you a more complete understanding of the material.

R—REMEMBERING

Once you have listened to the lecture, set the notes to paper, and translated/analyzed the material, it is time to study, or remember, the information. The next chapter on studying will assist you in this endeavor. Some of the best ways to remember information is to create a visual picture, speak the notes out loud, use mnemonic devices, and find a study partner. These techniques will be discussed in Chapter 7.

Putting It All Together: Note-Taking Techniques

There are as many systems and methods of note taking as there are people who take notes. Some people write too small, others too large. Some write too much, others not enough. Some write what is really important, while others miss key points. This section is provided to assist you in using the L-STAR system in a formalized note-taking technique. The L-STAR system can be used with any of the techniques about to be discussed.

Before we examine the three most commonly used note-taking systems, we need to review a few principles about basic note taking.

- Date your notes and use a heading.

- Keep notes from each class separate by using a divider or separate notebook system.

- Use the 8 1/2 x 11 paper with a three-hole punch.

- Copy any information that is written on the board, used on the overhead, or shown with charts and graphs.

- Organize and review your notes the same day as they are taken.

- Try not to "doodle" while taking notes.

- Use your own shorthand system.

- Clip related handouts to appropriate notes.

The three most common types of note-taking systems are

- Outline technique
- Cornell or Split-Page technique (also called the T system)
- Mapping technique

THE OUTLINE TECHNIQUE

While the outline technique is one of the most commonly used note-taking systems, it is also one of the most misused systems. Outlining your notes in class can be a difficult thing to do, especially if your professor does not follow an outline when lecturing. When using the outline system, it is best to get all the information from the lecture and then *combine* the lecture notes and text notes to create an outline after class. Most professors would not advise you to use the outline system of note taking in class. You may be able to use a modified outline while taking notes in class, but the most important thing to remember is not to get bogged down in a system; it is much more important that you concentrate on getting the ideas down on paper. You will always be able to go back after class and arrange your notes accordingly.

If you are going to use a modified or informal outline while taking class notes, you may want to consider grouping information together under a heading as a means of outlining. It is easier to remember information that is logically grouped than information that is scattered throughout the pages. If you are in an Economics class and the lecture is on taxes, you might outline your notes using the headings of Local Taxes, State Taxes, and Federal Taxes.

After you rewrite your notes using class lecture information and materials taken from the text, your note on the Process of Listening may look something like this:

```
Study Skills 101                    Oct. 17
                                    Wednesday
   Topic: Listening
   I. The Process of Listening (ROAR)
      A. R = Receiving
         1. W/in range of sound
         2. Hearing the information
      B. O = Organizing & focusing
         1. Choose to listen actively
         2. Observe the origin, direction & intent
      C. A = Assignment
         1. You assign a meaning
         2. May have to hear it more than once
      D. R = Reacting
         1. Our response to what we heard
         2. Reaction can be anything
   II. Definitions of Listening (POC)
      A. P = Listening w/ a purpose
      B. O = Listening w/ objectivity
      C. C = Listening constructively
```

THE CORNELL (MODIFIED CORNELL, SPLIT-PAGE OR T) SYSTEM

The Cornell System was developed by Dr. Walter Pauk of Cornell University. The basic principal of this system is to split the page into three sections. Each section will be used for different information. Section A will be used for questions that summarize information found in section B. Section B will be used for the actual notes from class, and section C will be used for a summary. Your blank note-taking page should look like the top example on the next page.

When using the Cornell method, you should choose a technique that is most comfortable and beneficial to you. You might use mapping (discussed later) or outlining on a Cornell page. A page of notes using an outline with the Cornell method will look like the bottom example on the next page.

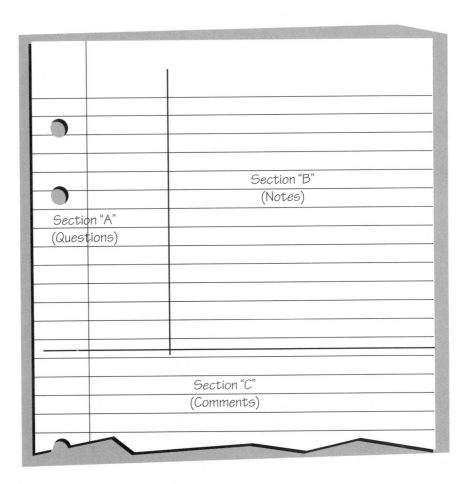

Section "B"
(Notes)

Section "A"
(Questions)

Section "C"
(Comments)

Study Skills 101   Oct. 19
Topic: Listening   Friday

	*The Listening Process or (ROAR)
	A = Receiving
What is	1. Within range of sound
the listening	2. Hearing the information
Process?	B = Organizing
(ROAR)	1. Choose to listen actively
	2. Observe origin
Definition	*Listening Defined
of Listening	A. Listening w/ a purpose
(POC)	B. Listening objectively
	C. Listening constructively
Obstacles	*What interferes w/ listening
(PTE)	A. Prejudging
	B. Talking
	C. Emotions

The listening process involves Receiving, Organizing, Assigning & Reacting - Talking, Prejudging & Emotions are obstacles.

THE MAPPING SYSTEM

If you are a visual learner, it might be important to review this section carefully. This note-taking system creates a picture of your information, and it may be easier to recall for those who learn best by visualization. The mapping system is just that; it creates a map or web of your information that allows you to see the relationship between certain facts, names, dates, and places. Your mapping system might look something like this:

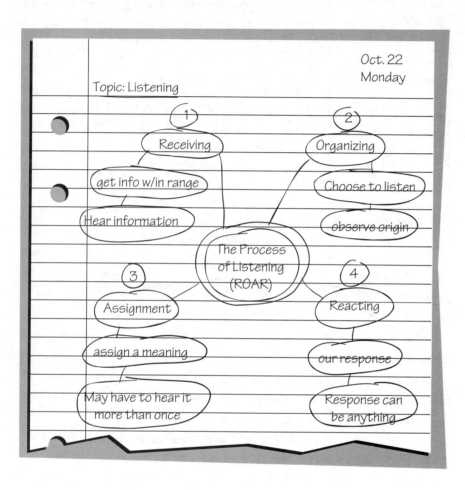

Mapping using the Cornell might resemble this illustration:

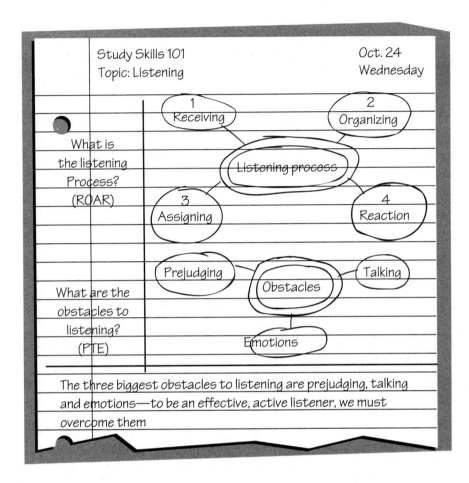

The most important thing to remember about each note-taking system is that it *must* work for you. Do not use a system because your friends use it or because you feel that you have to use a certain system. Experiment with each system to determine which is best for you. A combination might work best for you.

Always remember to keep your notes organized, dated, and neat. Notes that cannot be read are not good for you or anyone else. An example of a note-taking system that would probably be inappropriate for anyone is shown in the following illustration.

> *Tues.*
>
> **Greek Theater**
>
> • There were three playwrights in this era — Soph. Eur. & Aes. They utilized religious rituals & tried to bring about rebirth of crops by worshiping Dionysus
>
> Some of the best plays of the era were Oedipus, Oed. the King, Antigone — these were written by Sophocles. Eur. also wrote several plays.

Next, you will find a few questions that you need to ask yourself about your current note-taking system. After you have completed these questions, your professor will assign a lecture to which you should listen. Your professor will give you the details for taking notes in the spaces provided below. While listening to the lecture, you will need to take notes using the outline system, the Cornell system, and the mapping system. This is the only way to determine which is the most effective for you.

1. What system of note taking do you currently use?

_____
_____
_____

2. Does it work well? Why or why not?

_____
_____
_____

THE PROCESS OF NOTE TAKING

3. What advantages do you see in using the outline system?

_____
_____
_____

4. What advantages do you see in using the Cornell system?

_____
_____
_____

5. What advantages do you see in using the mapping system?

_____
_____
_____

Use the spaces provided below to practice your note-taking skills.

THE OUTLINE METHOD

_____
_____
_____
_____
_____
_____
_____
_____
_____
_____
_____
_____
_____

THE CORNELL METHOD

THE MAPPING METHOD

Roadways to Effective Note Taking

- Attend class.
- Be prepared for every class by doing homework assignments.
- Sit where you can see and hear the professor.
- Re-copy your notes after each class.
- If its on the board or overhead, write it down.
- Use loose-leaf paper.
- Keep your notes for each course separate.
- Keep good, straight posture when in class.
- Develop your listening abilities and tune out chatter.
- Ask questions.
- Use abbreviations and special notes to yourself.
- Keep your notes neat and clear; do not doodle on your notes.
- Participate in class.

Observations

If you remember the concepts of the L-STAR system (listening, setting it down, translating, analyzing, and remembering) and use this system as a study pattern and find a note-taking system that is comfortable and useful to you, then you will begin to see drastic changes in your abilities as a note taker and in your performance as a student.

As a Result of this Chapter, and in Preparing for My Journey, I Plan to . . .

CHAPTER 7

Driver Training
Learning How to Study

CHAPTER 7

The only man who is educated is the man who has learned how to learn: The man who has learned how to adapt and change: The man who has realized that no knowledge is secure, that only the process of seeking knowledge gives us a basis for security.

Carl Rogers

How well Lisa remembers her first semester in college. It was great being on her own. Everything was going well until her economics professor returned the first exam. She remembers it having twenty-five multiple-choice questions and three discussion questions. Lisa also remembered the shock she received when the test was returned with a failing grade. She was devastated! She couldn't believe it! She couldn't for the life of her figure out how it had happened. She remembers thinking/hoping that maybe her professor had made a mistake. Of course, he was correct. She remembers feeling scared and concerned about whether she should be in college.

There was a note on her exam from the professor that said to see him after class. With much fear, Lisa waited to speak to him after class. During their discussion, he shared with Lisa that he felt she hadn't studied for the test. Lisa explained that she had studied. She shared that she reviewed her class notes for almost an hour before the exam. He explained that an hour wasn't enough studying. He offered to work with her during his office hours. Lisa faithfully attended the study sessions, and she learned a variety of strategies designed to help her learn the material. At first, she was overwhelmed with the amount of study time, but as she became proficient in using studying skills, the amount of time she had to spend decreased. Even though Lisa only made a C in this class, she learned how to study. As a result, the classes she took after economics were much easier.

Homework? Studying? Who Needs It?

Some students think that homework and studying are merely writing or glancing at notes. This is a myth. Achieving success in school requires more than merely writing or glancing at notes. Unfortunately, many students are unsuccessful in school because they have never learned how to study.

In this chapter you will learn how to learn. It is extremely important that you keep an open mind when implementing the suggested techniques. You will be encouraged to try new things that will make a difference. Learning the skills, however, will require commitment, dedication, and time. The more you use the study skills, the better you will become at using them. Eventually, you will be able to spend less time and get better grades.

After completing this chapter, you will be able to

- Understand the importance of class attendance
- Explain and use various organizational strategies
- Use various textbook reading skills
- Apply techniques to learn vocabulary words
- Describe how to study math

For as long as you have been a student, you have had to study. The study habits you have developed during the years may be strong and effective, or they maybe weak and ineffective. Next, you will find ten questions intended to cause you to think about the effectiveness of your study skills.

SELF-STUDY

1. I am organized.
   1 2 3 4 5
2. I use a study plan.
   1 2 3 4 5
3. I know how to study math.
   1 2 3 4 5
4. I schedule a time to study.
   1 2 3 4 5
5. I know how to read a textbook. 1 2 3 4 5
6. I always attend class.
   1 2 3 4 5
7. I know how to learn vocabulary. 1 2 3 4 5
8. I know how to use an SQ3R approach when reading.
   1 2 3 4 5
9. I know how to highlight a textbook. 1 2 3 4 5
10. I have an appropriate place to study. 1 2 3 4 5

5=Strongly Agree
4=Agree
3=Don't Know
2=Disagree
1=Strongly Disagree

TOTAL YOUR POINTS After you total your points from these ten questions, use the following chart to analyze your score.

0–10   Your study skill techniques are poor.

11–20 Your study skill techniques are below average.

21–30 Your study skill techniques are average.

31–40 Your study skill techniques are above average.

41–50 Your study skill techniques are excellent.

How did you do? Does your score represent what you know about yourself? If your score is a concern, relax. This chapter is designed to teach basic study skill techniques.

Attending Class

Studying includes being organized and knowing and using a variety of study techniques. Before we begin discussing these skills, we must discuss the importance of attending class. Some students fail to take class attendance seriously. Attending class is crucial for studying to be effective. Your instructor will guide you through your studying journey. By providing course outlines, instructions, and suggestions, instructors help you to achieve success in their courses. By making every attempt to attend class, you are ensuring your success. If you are unable to attend class, you are still responsible for the information covered.

Getting Organized

To do a good job of studying, you have to be organized. You will need to develop a notebook system that allows you to store class notes, handouts, and assignments. Being organized also involves having an appropriate study environment, having accessible study supplies, planning a time to study, and developing a study plan.

What Notebook Systems Do You Use?

It would be very difficult to study the material in a history class if you do not record what was presented during class. Taking notes during class gives you valuable information to review or study prior to an exam. Chapter 6 thoroughly addresses the appropriate notebook system and gives you information about how to take notes.

When Do You Study?

To study effectively, you must set aside a time specifically for the purpose of studying. If you fail to schedule a time to study, you will most likely not have enough time to study. Since it is recommended that students spend two hours studying for every one hour in class (this varies from student to student), organizing your time is critical. Chapter 3, Time Management, discusses how to manage time effectively.

Where Do You Study?

Choosing the best study environment can determine how successful you will be when you are studying. The appropriate study place is different for everyone. It needs to be a place where you are comfortable. Therefore, paying attention to the physical condition of the room is important. Proper lighting and temperature, for instance, should be considered. When the lights are low and the room is warm, you may have an urge to take a nap. Some students also need some degree of noise in the background to concentrate and others do not. It is therefore okay to play soft music when studying. But, choose a station or tape that is either classical or pop or a type of music to which you normally do not listen, because the inclination is to listen to your favorite music while you study. When you are at home, you should choose a room that is quiet and free of distractions. Perhaps the dining room table or your bedroom might be a good choice, provided that your bedroom has a desk where you can work. If you find that you cannot concentrate at home, then you should identify a place outside of your home for studying. A great choice is the school library or student study center.

Describe your study environment. _____

_____

_____

_____

Do you feel your study place is appropriate? Why or why not? _____
_____
_____
_____
_____

List potential study environments that you could use. _____
_____
_____
_____
_____

Study Supplies

Once you have identified where you plan to do most of your studying, the next step is to be prepared for studying. Each time you study, you should have all of your study supplies at hand. It is amazing how much time is wasted when you are not prepared. Therefore, you should have everything you regularly use in a portable basket or box. Your study supplies should include, but not be limited to, the following items:

- Pencils
- Sharpener
- Notebook paper
- Staples
- Thesaurus
- Index cards
- Scientific calculator
- Pens
- Highlighters
- Stapler
- Folders

Dictionary

Colored pencils

Paper clips

List additional supplies that you feel you would need. _____
_____
_____
_____

A Study Plan

Now that you have chosen a notebook system, decided on a place to study, placed all of your study supplies in a basket, and identified specific times for studying, you must create a study plan. Making a to-do list will help you organize your study time. This plan will enable you to get the most from your valuable time. List first the most difficult assignments to be completed. If you save those items until the end, you will not be at your best when you are doing them. By waiting until the end to complete difficult tasks, your frustration will be increased and you may decide not to complete the assignments. If you do not complete everything on your list, the unfinished work should be transferred to your study plan for the next day.

Using the academic subjects that you are taking this semester, create a study plan using the following to-do list.

TO-DO LIST

1. _____
2. _____
3. _____
4. _____
5. _____

Learning is not a task or a problem—it is a way to be in the world. Man learns as he pursues goals and projects that have meaning for him.

Sidney Journard

Roadways of Studying

The roadways of studying involves getting organized and then studying. The first step is to be *organized*. The tips mentioned at the beginning of this chapter describe ways to become organized. The second step is to *study*. Studying is what you do to learn a new skill and to reinforce prior knowledge. The remainder of this chapter will focus on five areas:

1. Learning vocabulary
2. Reading and using textbooks
3. Reviewing class and textbook notes
4. Studying math
5. Identifying tips for studying effectively

Learning Vocabulary

You need to have an understanding of words in order to effectively communicate with those around you. How well you speak, write, read, and understand words determines how successful you can be in school.

Students with weak vocabularies are at a disadvantage. These students have trouble understanding their college textbooks and their instructors' class lectures. It is, therefore, important that you make a commitment to build your vocabulary.

Perhaps one of the best strategies to improve vocabulary and reading comprehension is (to put it simply) *reading*. When you read, it is crucial that you not skip over the words that are unfamiliar to you. Doing so effects your ability to understand what you have read. Instead, use *context clues* and *word analysis* to define the unfamiliar words.

CONTEXT CLUES

The sentence or paragraph that a word appears in is known as the context of the word. The words around the unfamiliar word can be very helpful in identifying the meaning of a word. For instance, what does the word *capricious* mean? By itself it may be difficult to define the word; however, in the following sentence the word may seem clear: "Her capricious or impulsive nature caused her to make many mistakes." In this context, the word *capricious* means "acting impulsively." The sentence itself defines the meaning of the word.

Context clues usually give you a vague meaning for a word and allow you to continue your reading without stopping to look up a word in a dictionary. There are three basic context clues that you can look for as you read through the sentence and/or paragraph.

- One context clue that a sentence can offer is a definition of the word. In fact, it may actually define the unfamiliar word. An example would be *palatial*: "The apartment was so spacious and beautiful it could be called *palatial*."

- Another clue to look for in the context is opposition. In this case, the context may explain what the word does *not* mean. An example of this would be the word *egocentric*: "She was not *egocentric*, because she cared deeply for other people."

- The third clue to look for in the context is an example of what the word means. Here the context gives you another word for the word used. An example of this would be *horticulture*. *Horticulture,* or gardening, has become a very popular way to reduce stress.

You may find that using context clues when reading helps you to understand what you have read and limits the interruption of having to look in a dictionary. The dictionary is a valuable resource and should be used when you cannot determine the meaning of a word. It is also a good idea to highlight the unfamiliar words in your dictionary and/or put the word and its definition on index cards.

Practice using context clues to define the word indicated in each of the following sentences.

1. Many kinesthetic *learners find that they must move during the learning process.* Kinesthetic *means* _____

2. It's amazing that John is always immaculately *dressed, yet his car is often dirty.* Immaculate *means* _____

3. *I was* mortified *or embarrassed when my voice cracked during my speech.* Mortified *means* _____

4. *Lisa* procrastinates *instead of getting her work done on time.* Procrastinates *means* _____

5. *You can save money by buying* generic *brands of food.* Generic *means* _____

6. *The South's warm and sunny climate is very* hospitable, *or comfortable, to many Northerners.* Hospitable *means* _____

WORD ANALYSIS

Another technique that can be used to decode an unfamiliar word is word analysis. Word analysis involves examining parts of a word to determine its meaning. Words can be made up of roots or base words, prefixes that come before the base word, and/or suffixes, which come after the base word. An example would be the word *disconnection*.

- The root of this word is *connect*.
- The prefix of this word is *dis*.
- The suffix of this word *tion*.

Becoming familiar with common prefixes and suffixes can help you when you come across an unfamiliar word.

Some common prefixes are

Prefix	Meaning	Example
un	not	unusual
in	not	incomplete
pre	before	prenuptial
post	after	posttest
re	again	restart

Some common suffixes are

Suffix	Meaning	Example
ness	full of	usefulness
less	lack of	useless

ful	full of	hopeful
able	full of	knowledgeable
ward	in the direction of	backward

Reading and Using Textbooks

Every textbook is filled with a variety of features designed to guide you through the material you are reading. To successfully use your textbooks, you will need to become familiar with all the features in your textbooks. Every time you receive or purchase a new textbook, you should spend twenty to thirty minutes becoming familiar with the special features of the text, such as a table of contents or glossary.

An example of a table of contents with special features is shown on the next page.

PART VII ■ EDUCATIONAL AND VOCATIONAL

 15 Education and School 373

TRENDS IN AMERICAN EDUCATION 373
Traditionalists versus Progressives 373
Rise of Progressive Education 374
Sputnik and After 375
1960s and 1970s 375
1980s 375
1990s 376

ADOLESCENTS VIEW THEIR SCHOOLS 376
Students Grade Their Schools 376
Quality of Teachers 377
Teachers as Significant Others 378

 HIGHLIGHT
Traditional versus Generative Instruction 378

Student Responsibility 378

THE SECONDARY SCHOOL TEACHER 379
What Makes a Teacher? 379
Personality Traits and Character 379
Teachers' Relationship with Others 380
Professional Qualifications 380

CURRICULUM CONSIDERATIONS 381
Three Curricula 381
Curriculum Improvement 381

MIDDLE SCHOOLS 382

PRIVATE VERSUS PUBLIC SCHOOLS 383

 HIGHLIGHT
Tracking 383

ACHIEVEMENT AND DROPPING OUT 385
Enrollment Figures 385
Who Drops Out and Why 385
Truancy 387
Socioeconomic Factors 387

Ethnic Considerations 387
Family Relationships 388
Personality Characteristics 389
Social Adjustment, Peer Associations 390
Employment, Money 390
School Stress 390
School Failure, Apathy, Dissatisfaction 390
Alienation 391
Pregnancy, Marriage 392

 HIGHLIGHT
Middle-Class Parenting
and Underachievement 392

SUMMARY 393

KEY TERMS 394

THOUGHT QUESTIONS 394

SUGGESTED READING 395

 16 Work and Vocation 397

MOTIVES FOR CHOICE 397

THEORIES OF VOCATIONAL CHOICE 399
Ginzberg's Compromise with Reality Theory 399

 HIGHLIGHT
Developmental–Contextual Concepts 401

Holland's Occupational Environment Theory 402

HIGHLIGHT
Career Classes 402

PEOPLE INFLUENCING CHOICE 403
Parents 403

 PERSONAL ISSUES
Career Indecision and
Family Enmeshment 404

Peers 405
School Personnel 405

List the features most commonly found in a textbook.

_____

_____

_____

Your list should include the following: table of contents, chapter headings and subheadings, key vocabulary words, section questions, chapter introductions and summaries, study questions, glossary, index, appendix, preface, and so on.

Using one of your textbooks, list the some of the features and their purpose.

Feature _____

Purpose _____

_____

Feature _____

Purpose _____

_____

Feature _____

Purpose _____

_____

Feature _____

Purpose _____

_____

The SQ3R Method

After you have previewed your textbook, reviewed the table of contents, and identified chapter features, it is time to begin reading and learning the chapter information. Some students find reading textbook material difficult. One of the best ways to read, learn, and study a chapter in your textbook is to use the SQ3R method. This stands for:

S—Survey

Q—Question

R—*Read*

R—*Recite*

R—*Review*

The process for using the SQ3R method is as follows.

STEP 1: SURVEY

The first step of the SQ3R method involves surveying or prereading the assigned chapter in your textbook. You begin surveying by reading the title and introduction of the chapter. This information gives you an overview of the chapter. As you survey the chapter, read the headings, subheadings, and key vocabulary (usually in bold print), and look at the graphs, tables, and pictures. Finally, read the chapter summary and the review questions. After surveying the chapter, you should be familiar with the information. Reading, learning, and studying the chapter becomes easier when you take fifteen to twenty minutes to survey the contents.

STEP 2: QUESTION

The second step of the SQ3R method is to form questions. Take each heading and subheading and turn it into a question. Questions beginning with "why," "what," or "how" are the most effective ones. Creating questions establishes a purpose for reading and will enable you to stay focused.

STEP 3: READ

The third step of the SQ3R method is to read with the purpose of finding the answers to the questions you have formed. Do not read passively. Become actively involved in what you are reading by highlighting key phrases that answer your questions and by making notes in the margin. When you read actively, you are reading effectively.

STEP 4: RECITE

The next step in this method is to recite what you have learned. After you have read the entire chapter, go back and recite the answers to the questions. This strategy is an important step in remembering what you have read.

STEP 5: REVIEW

The final step in the SQ3R method is to review the entire chapter. This step is very similar to surveying. Once again, go back and read the introduction, headings, subheadings, vocabulary, the special notes that you made in the margins or text, the summary questions, and the study questions. Any questions you still cannot answer or information that is not clear should be noted so that you can ask your instructor for clarification.

The SQ3R method is a thorough way to read, to study, and to learn new information. If you complete all the steps in the SQ3R method, you will, in all likelihood, be thoroughly learning the material—the desired outcome. You will be amazed at how easy it is to understand your textbooks when you use the SQ3R technique. The results will be far reaching: You feel more prepared for class, class lectures will be clearer and easier, and most of all, your performance on tests will improve.

Highlighting Your Textbook

Highlighting your textbook or an article is a technique to use when you are reading, learning, and studying. Keep the following suggestions in mind when highlighting:

1. Highlight approximately one third of a paragraph (main ideas and supporting details).

2. Label main ideas and supporting details by using different colored highlighters.

3. Make margin notes using special notations such as RR for re-read; DEF for definition; 1, 2, 3 for enumeration; and !!!/*** for important.

4. Take notes on highlighted chapters and add them to your class notes.

5. *Never* rely on highlighting that someone else has done in *your* text.

Practicing the SQ3R

A sample chapter from *Understanding Plays* (1994), by Millie Barranger, is found on pages 19–23. Using this sample, practice using the SQ3R method; then answer the questions.

Survey the following chapter.

1. What is the title of the chapter? _____
2. How many major headings are found in this chapter? _____
3. Are there any graphs, tables, or pictures? _____
4. Is there a chapter summary? _____

Form **questions** from the chapter.

1. Choose three of the headings and turn them into questions for review.

a. _____

b. _____

c. _____

Read the chapter, highlighting key phrases.

1. What is the answer to question (a) above? _____
_____

2. What is the answer to question (b) above? _____
_____

3. What is the answer to question (c) above? _____
_____

Recite the answers to the questions you asked earlier, without referring to notes.

Jot down your notes: _____
_____
_____

Review the entire chapter.

1. Where were plays first analyzed? _____
_____

2. What is dramatic *space*? _____

_____

_____

3. What is dramatic *time*? _____

_____

_____

4. What is a *dramaturg*? _____

_____

Understanding Plays

The manuscript, the words on the page, was what you started with and what you have left. The production is of great importance, has given the play the life it will know, but it is gone, in the end, and the pages are the only wall against which to throw the future or measure the past.

—Lillian Hellman[1]

DRAMA AND PERFORMANCE

We are bombarded daily with television, videos, newsprint, films, and dramatic events. Terrorists threaten the lives of airline passengers, battles are fought in faraway places, nations negotiate peace treaties, nuclear accidents threaten lives, and a famous boxer divorces his glamorous actress-wife. All are subjects for novels, films, miniseries, and plays. The larger subject is human experience (real or imagined), but the means of representing experience in artistic forms differ with the artist and with the medium. A play, or the dramatic text, is one of the theatre's principal media. It is at once a text to be read and a script to be performed.

Plays are read daily by individuals as diverse as stage directors, designers, actors, technicians, teachers, students, critics, scholars, and the general public. In contrast to novels and poetry, a play is often the most difficult type of prose or poetry to read because it is written not only to be read, but also to be performed by actors before audiences. Like a screenplay, a play is also given life by actors although the medium and technology are significantly different. Kevin Kline acts Shakespeare's Hamlet or Derek Jacobi performs Richard II on a stage before audiences for the time of the performance. In contrast, their film performances in *The Big Chill* and *I, Claudius*, respectively, are contained, unchanging, on videotape for all time.

Reading plays is a unique challenge. As readers, we must visualize all of the elements the playwright has placed on the page to convey a story to us: its characters in action and conflict, its happening in time and space, and, at the end, the completed meaning of all that has happened.

Plays have been formally analyzed since the days of classical Greece. Aristotle's *Poetics* (c. 330 B.C.) is our first record of a critical assessment of plays presented in the ancient Greek festivals. Since Aristotle, there have been many approaches to "understanding" plays. For our purposes, we will approach the analysis of plays from the viewpoint and techniques of the playwright who creates the dramatic text. As Lillian Hellman said, the words on the page are the playwright's measure, after all is said and done, of the future and the past: "The manuscript, the words on the page, was what you started with and what you have left."[2]

Although we call the playwright's words on the printed page "drama," we also use the words "drama" and "dramatic" to describe many events ranging from riots to parades, from sports events to political speeches. That these current events are "real" rather than "fiction" is the essential distinction between life's "dramas" and dramatic "texts." Martin Esslin wrote that "a dramatic text, unperformed, is literature."[3] Like a novel or poem, drama, as written words, is considered a literary text. The chief ingredient that distinguishes drama from other types of literature is, precisely, its potential for being performed or enacted. The very origin of the word "drama" implies its potential for becoming a performable script. We use the words "text" or "script" to describe this written form that becomes the basis for theatrical performance.

Drama comes from the Greek *dran*, meaning "to do" or "to act." Since the word

4

is rooted in "doing" or "enacting," we have come to understand drama as a special way of imitating human behavior and human events. Drama is like narrative in that it tells a story; but unlike narrative, or story telling, it requires enactment before an audience. The story's events must be represented in drama, not merely told or narrated as in epic poetry. The word *"theatre"* has its roots in the Greek word, *theatron,* meaning "a place for seeing," or that special place where actors and audiences come together to experience a performance of the playwright's raw materials—the drama. The dramatic text is not wholly realized until the theatre's artists complete for audiences what the playwright began. As Hamlet, Kenneth Branaugh must breathe life into Shakespeare's character for the text to come alive in the imagined world of Elsinore Castle.

All dramatic texts are constructs. They have in common the fact that they set forth events taking place in an imagined or fictional world, whether it be ancient Thebes or contemporary Manhattan. The dramatic text is the playwright's blueprint for setting forth physical and psychological experience—to give shape and meaning to the world as the playwright sees and understands it. Over the centuries, these blueprints have related a variety of stories not as narrations, but as imitations of imaginary actions. Sophocles wrote of a king confronted by a plague-ridden kingdom (*Oedipus the King*), Sam Shepard depicted American midwesterners confronting their lost connections with the land and with one another (*Buried Child*), and Samuel Beckett presented worlds in which human beings "wait out" lifetimes (*Footfalls*).

Drama, then, is a special written way of imitating human experience. It is both a literary and a performance text. The fictional character, Hamlet, is played by the living actor Kevin Kline. It is our purpose here to learn to *read* plays, to understand the how and why of the dramatic text, without ignoring the fact that the playwright's words have the potential to be performed in the theatre. We must learn to analyze the pattern of words and conventions that have the potential for "becoming" living words and actions. The playwright provides us with dialogue—words arranged in a meaningful sequence—intended to be spoken aloud and enacted by actors before audiences. Often the playwright includes descriptions of scenes, characters, and activities in stage directions and dialogue. However, the actor remains the playwright's essential intermediary in that complex relationship between the drama and the performance.

DRAMATURGY

In its original Greek meaning, a *dramaturg* was simply a playwright. The word "dramaturgy" defines the playwright's craft. It involves the elements, conventions, and techniques the playwright uses to delineate general and particular truths about the human condition. Those elements involve plot, action, character, meaning, language, spectacle, space, and time. We must develop skills for understanding a writer's dramaturgical skills, which deal with plot, character, language, and so forth, so that we can read plays from all periods of theatrical, cultural, and social history. Styles, conventions, language, and techniques differ among playwrights depending on the physical theatre, the writing conventions of the historical period, and the society or universe mirrored in the writer's work. Also applicable are the ever-changing cultural, social, and technological conditions under which plays have been written, produced, and performed in western society for 2500 years.

DRAMATIC SPACE

Drama is unique among the arts in that it imitates reality through representation rather than narration. The playwright creates a fictional universe with human beings, familiar objects, and recognizable environments. Beckett's characters' feet hurt; August Wilson's hero idolizes his baseball bat; Shepard's Dodge lives out his last days on a frayed green sofa surrounded by pills and whiskey bottles. Like Beckett, Wilson, and Shepard, playwrights use "real" human beings in particular spaces and times to create the illusion of fictional worlds in which recognizable events take place in time and space. We distinguish between the *performance space* (the stage) and the *dramatic space* (the playwright's fictional locale). Dramatic space—or the play's environment—is usually described in dialogue or in stage directions found in modern texts. What is exhibited in the performance space is an interpretation, or staging, of the play's physical requirements set forth in those directions.

Dramatic space has essentially two characteristics. First, it is a "fictional" space—the characters' environment—described by playwrights in dialogue and stage directions. The fictional space may be the palace of Thebes (*Oedipus the King*), an eighteenth-century drawing room (*The School for Scandal*), or the neglected living room of a modern midwestern family (*Buried Child*). The fictional space may encompass simultaneously more than one space, such as palaces and battlefields or apartments and streets. Shakespeare's plays require locations that are miles apart, but the characters must appear in those locales within seconds. Hamlet moves from battlements, to chambers, to graveyards. Dramatic space is magical in its ability to present several locales simultaneously. Bertolt Brecht's Galileo travels many miles and journeys to many cities in his pursuit of truth and reason.

Second, dramatic space always assumes the presence of a stage and an audience and a relationship between the two. As we read plays, we are aware that they are written to be performed. While the stage where a play is produced may be almost any type—proscenium, arena, thrust, environmental—the characters may or may not be aware of the audience. In modern realistic plays, the characters are not aware that an audience is present. The pretense, or stage convention, is that a "fourth wall" exists through which the actors-as-characters cannot see, although audiences can. No character in Henrik Ibsen's *Hedda Gabler* ever acknowledges the audience. In other plays, characters directly address the audience, establishing an invisible flow of space between actor and audience. Sheridan's *The School for Scandal* has many asides where characters speak directly to the audience to comment briefly on some situation. As readers, we need to be sensitive to the "look" of the characters' environment and to the intended relationship of the dramatic space to the audience.

DRAMATIC TIME

Dramatic time is a phenomenon of the text. Jan Kott wrote that "theatre is a place where time is always present."[4] Once begun, the time of a performance is one-directional. It follows a linear path for the two or more hours of its duration. Dramatic time, in contrast to performance time, is free of such constraints.

Within the fictional world of the play, time can be expanded or compressed. Unlike the film editor's manipulation of images in films, the playwright does not have the advantage of editing and splicing film to carry us forward or backward in time. Rather, dramatic time can be accelerated by using gaps of days, months, and even years; or, it can be slowed down by using soliloquies and flashbacks. Whereas real or performance time moves in one direction (present to future) and the past can never be recaptured, dramatic time can violate the relentless forward motion of performance time measured by the clock. For example, events may be shown out of their chronological sequence, or they may be foreshortened so they occur more swiftly than they would in nature. Shakespeare's battles, requiring only a few minutes of swordplay on stage, would ordinarily require days or even months in real time. In Samuel Beckett's plays, characters experience the relentless passage of time because there are no major events or crises. An unchanging sameness characterizes their lives. In Samuel Beckett's *Waiting for Godot*, Vladimir and Estragon wait for Godot's arrival which is always postponed by the messenger's announcement that "Mr. Godot told me to tell you he won't come this evening but surely tomorrow." In Beckett's plays the experience of dramatic time is cyclical—day becomes night and night becomes day—while his characters wait out their uneventful lives in patterns that are repetitive and are experienced as "waiting." In his plays, nothing happens in the traditional sense, but time erodes lives in a relentless journey toward death.

Time and space in the fictional universe of drama are highly malleable and unlike the actual time we experience in our daily lives. Consideration of dramatic time and space has always played a large part in the different theories and rules of drama. In his *Poetics*, Aristotle briefly suggested that the amount of time it takes the actors to tell the story should ideally be concurrent with the actual time it takes to perform the play. This attention to a *unity of time*, as it was later called, is still found in modern realistic plays. However, in the many words written about drama over the centuries, the most attention has been given to the playwright's meanings and messages.

DRAMA'S MEANINGS AND MESSAGES

The reader's greatest temptation is to concentrate on the general meaning of the literary work—the novel, poem, or play—overlooking the fact that meaning is generated as the work is experienced. A play's complete meaning does not emerge in the early pages of a text or in the first moments of a performance, but quite often the seeds of the message can be found there. Shepard's statement about the decay of American family values is evident in the first moments of *Buried Child*.

In creating the dramatic text, the playwright connects the reader (and audiences) with a common humanity through the progression of the play's events. Great plays confront us with life's verities, conveying the hope, courage, despair, compassion, violence, love, hate, exploitation, and generosity experienced by all humankind. They show us the possibilities of losing our families and property through accidents, catastrophes of war, or tyranny. Plays show us ways of fulfilling ourselves in relationships or confronting despair and death. August Wilson's characters struggle to show love and affection to one another. The most enduring plays explore what it means to be human beings in special circumstances. These circumstances may be unfamiliar, like the prince dispossessed of his rightful heritage through murder, marriage, and calumny (*Hamlet*); or bizarre, like the family that has literally buried its family skeleton in the back yard (*Buried Child*); or familiar, like the ambitions of a mother for her children (*The Glass Menagerie*).

Drama's most enduring achievements, like the representative plays contained in this book, serve as reflections of ourselves, or what potentially could be ourselves in different times and circumstances. Drama's best moments lead us to discoveries and reflections about our personalities, circumstances, desires, anxieties, hopes, and dreams. Playwrights also move beyond personal concerns to discuss social and political issues that are of a certain time, yet transcend specific historical periods. Playwrights stimulate social awareness and put us in touch with our thoughts and feelings about issues. The aim of great playwrights is to expand our consciousness on old and new social and personal issues, and to endow us with *new perspectives* on our humanity and the human condition.

Plays are written as a process of unfolding and discovery. To read plays successfully is to understand essentially "how" the playwright generates meaning. Scene follows scene in meaningful patterns; dialogue communicates feelings and ideas; characters display motives and emotions; locales give social and economic contexts. "What" a play means involves the completed action, that is, all that has gone before in organized, meaningful segments that, when taken in their totality, express the writer's vision or conviction about the world. As readers, we share that unfolding—those discoveries—with audiences. We also learn to experience the developing actions, events, and relationships which, in turn, produce a coherent statement about individuals, societies, and the universe. We learn to follow the playwright's ways and means of organizing the dramatic material into a coherent whole and to discover the writer's methods for developing the psychological and physical currents of human endeavor that result in visible (and meaningful) behavior.

The same process is at work in our personal experiences. In our daily lives, we are not instantly aware that some actions have repercussions far beyond our expectations. As we begin a trip, we cannot know the full extent of our experiences. With time, we come to understand the meaning of our experiences, feelings, and actions, as well as the motives and actions of others. In some instances, meanings are elusive—sometimes impossible to pin down. The same is true in understanding the how and the why of the dramatic text. When Tom Wingfield brings the "gentleman caller" to dine with his sister Laura in Tennessee Williams' *The Glass Menagerie,* he is not aware, nor are we as readers and audiences, of the psychological damage he is imposing on Laura's fragile emotional life.

All art condenses, clarifies, and orders the chaos, disorder, and inconsequential happenings of life. The poet William Wordsworth gives shape to girlhood innocence in his "Lucy Gray" poems. Tennessee Williams organizes Tom Wingfield's memories of his chaotic and unhappy life in his mother's home. However, great plays confront life's complexities in such a way that they cannot be reduced to a single meaning. Since there is usually no author's voice in drama, as there is in the novel where the writer can speak directly to the reader, we are left with layers of possible meaning based on the play's events. We can usually agree that Hamlet was given the task of avenging his father's murder, that he hesitated and ultimately achieved his objective at the cost of his life. What remains open to interpretation is the ultimate meaning or significance of the play—"what it was all about." For that reason, we can read and see *Hamlet* any number of times and continue to discover new meanings in this complex text. We want to learn to identify *how* playwrights order, clarify, and distill their imitations of real life in the dramatic text and what higher meanings emerge from these efforts.

Sam Shepard's Pulitzer-Prize-winning *Buried Child* (1978) is an interesting contemporary play with which to begin our process of understanding plays. Along with a post-Vietnam wave of American writers that includes David Mamet, Marsha Norman, Lanford Wilson, August Wilson, and many others, Shepard takes us into the inner workings of modern American family life which are both commonplace and bizarre. He writes about characters searching out their family histories in an effort to explain who they are and how they came to be that way. Similar to *Oedipus the King* and *Hamlet,* the central action of *Buried Child* is the individual's quest for roots and identity. Shepard's means of organizing and unfolding a family's history provide our initial introduction to play analysis. Let us begin this journey into the process of understanding plays with *Buried Child.*

Reviewing Class and Textbook Notes

An effective study skill strategy is *review*. Reviewing your class notes (you may even want to re-copy them) and the textbook notes regularly will certainly help you become more successful as a student.

Strategies for note taking were discussed in Chapter 6. Each time you sit down to study, the first thing that you should do is review what you last studied. This is a very important critical thinking skill that will assist you in seeing the whole picture. Just as warming up prepares you for exercising, reviewing your notes prepares you for studying. If you study each assignment without reviewing prior lessons, you will have difficulty seeing the relationship between new lessons and assignments.

One way to review class and textbook notes is to write a summary of what you have learned. This activity should be done on loose-leaf paper and added to your class notes. Writing a summary should take you only fifteen to twenty minutes. Use the following questions to help guide you through your summary:

1. What are four important facts that I learned in class and/or while reading my textbook?

2. What are four associations I can make about today's class notes or reading assignments that relate to previous notes?

Writing a summary can make preparing for exams much easier. This is also an excellent way to remember what you are studying, because you are thoroughly learning the material. Thoroughly learning is the key to remembering information.

Using notes from a class you are currently taking, answer the following questions:

1. What are four important facts that you learned in class and/or while reading your textbook?

a. _____

b. _____

c. _____
d. _____

2. What are four associations you can make about today's class notes or reading assignments that relate to previous notes?

a. _____
b. _____
c. _____
d. _____

Studying Math

Do you dislike numbers? Are you terrified of math? If so, you are not alone. Academic counselors tell us that of the students who seek academic counseling, most express anxiety related to math.

Many students will avoid math at all costs. They will put off taking math courses until the last possible semester. Some students will even go as far as choosing degrees that require little or no math. Unfortunately, the fear or anxiety that students suffer can determine whether they will earn the degrees they pursue.

The first step in studying math is to overcome to the best of your ability the anxiety you have about math. Let us begin by identifying what has caused the math anxiety or fear. List some reasons why you dislike math or suffer from math anxiety:

_____
_____
_____
_____
_____
_____

> *You can choose to throw stones, to stumble on them, to climb over them, or to build with them.*
>
> **William Arthur Ward**

Your list might include being embarrassed by a peer or teacher, conflict with teacher, family pressure, desires to be perfect, poor teaching methods, you feel you don't have a "math mind," you have heard that only men can do math, and so forth.

Your reasons for fearing math are legitimate, but it is important that you let go of the past. The negative thoughts that you carry around with you are keeping you from reaching your math potential. Some math instructors feel that the students who don't learn to control their math anxiety, won't be able to be academically successful in math.

How you study math is different from how you might study history, for which you may need only to listen and take notes during class and review your notes outside of class. Math, on the the other hand, requires a great deal more. You should not only listen and take notes during class, but also practice the math concepts outside of class. Learning and studying math requires a great deal of time, paper-and-pencil activity, patience, and determination. You need to be committed to daily drill and review. Math concepts build on top of each other. If you do not build a good foundation, you will struggle with later concepts. For example, it is very important that you learn and understand the concept of least common multiples (LCM), because finding the LCM of two unlike denominators will allow you to add or subtract the fractions.

Listed next you will find several practical suggestions for studying math. If you want to experience success with math, you must be willing to implement or use as many of these suggestions as possible.

- Purchase a student solutions manual.
- Learn relaxation techniques to control math anxiety.
- Read the directions carefully.
- Ask yourself if your answer makes sense.
- Redo problems to reinforce understanding and to check.
- Use a scientific calculator if permitted.
- Ask your instructor about what math teaching aids are available on your campus, such as videos, computer tutor, math hotline number, and so on.
- Hire a tutor.
- Create a math study group.

- Copy all examples that the instructor puts on the board.
- Above all, practice, practice, practice.

ROADWAYS TO STUDYING EFFECTIVELY

- **Become organized.**
- **Create and use a notebook system.**
- **Identify an appropriate study environment and study time.**
- **Create and use a study plan.**
- **Use the SQ3R studying method.**
- **Thoroughly learn material.**
- **Use mnemonic devices.**
- **Summarize class and textbook notes.**
- **Use context clues and word analysis to define unfamiliar words.**
- **Use the tips recommended to study math effectively.**
- **Use index cards for vocabulary, formulas, concepts, and so on.**
- **Above all, study over a period of time.** *Do not cram!*

Live as if you were to die tomorrow. Learn as if you were to live forever.

M.K. Gandhi

Observations

Learning how to learn is an important step in achieving academic success. The strategies mentioned in this chapter will require commitment, determination, and time. You can reach your educational potential by becoming organized and implementing the study techniques covered in this chapter. We must look to the old saying, "If you give a man food, you feed him once. If you teach him to plant, you nourish him forever." The same is true with learning. If you learn *how* to learn, you can learn forever!

As a Result of this Chapter, and in Preparing for My Journey, I Plan to . . .

CHAPTER 8

Obtaining Your License
Test-Taking Strategies

CHAPTER 8

No one can make you feel inferior without your consent.
Eleanor Roosevelt, former U.S. First Lady

Ann, a thirty-five-year old single mother of three, decided to go back to school in order to make a better life for herself and her children. She wanted a better job, but she didn't have the skills needed to get one.

For ten years she had worked as a secretary in a small law office and enjoyed working in the legal system. So, she decided to apply for admission into the paralegal curriculum at the local community college. She enrolled as a night student and decided to take just one course her first semester. Her advisor encouraged her to take PSY 201, a general requirement for her degree.

The semester seemed to be going fine until her instructor announced the first test date. Ann was horrified of tests. She'd never been very good at taking a test. She knew that if she didn't overcome her fear, she'd never be able to earn a degree and create a better life for herself and family.

With determination, Ann began studying three weeks prior to the exam. She put all her notes on large index cards, and she divided the index cards into six different groups. She carried the cards with her everywhere she went. Ann studied and studied and studied.

On the day of the exam, she felt confident that she could pass it. She completed the first part of the exam without much trouble. It wasn't until Ann attempted to answer the essay that a wave of anxiety came over her. She remembers feeling very hot, realizing that her hands were sweating, and feeling overwhelmed. Ann's mind had gone blank. She didn't know how to answer the essay. She didn't know where to begin. This was a timed test, and the time was running out. Ann remembers wanting to give up, crawl into a corner, and cry.

She must have wasted fifteen minutes trying to get under control. Finally, she decided to write anything that came to her mind. She decided just to do the best that she could. Ann was amazed at how easy it started to come to her after she took control of the anxiety. Because she had prepared for the exam and thoroughly learned the material, Ann was able to finish the test with confidence. At the next class meeting, she learned that she passed the exam. Ann was so relieved and proud. The hard work had paid off, and she knew she was going to make it!

It is natural to be nervous or anxious about taking tests. When we take tests, the result will be either a passing or a failing grade. It is the fear of failure that creates the anxiety. Students can increase their ability to succeed and decrease the anxiety by becoming "testwise." Preparing for tests, knowing how to control test anxiety, and understanding the types of tests will make taking tests, if not a positive experience, at least not a negative one. This chapter will teach you how to take tests. It is important that you understand that the tips and techniques discussed in this chapter should not take the place of studying for a test. The best way to be successful when taking a test is to learn the material thoroughly and have a positive attitude.

At the end of this chapter, if you complete the exercises, participate in class, read additional assignments issued by your instructor, and keep an open mind, you will be able to complete the following tasks:

- Explain the purpose of tests
- Describe how to control test anxiety
- Use tips for reducing test anxiety
- Apply general test-taking techniques
- Use strategies for answering various types of test questions

You have been taking tests your entire academic life, but how "testwise" are you? Next, you will find ten questions intended to cause you to think about the purpose of tests, about test anxiety, and about how to take various types of tests. Take a moment and respond to each statement.

SELF-STUDY

1. I am relaxed when taking a test.   *1 2 3 4 5*
2. I am always physically and mentally ready to take a test.   *1 2 3 4 5*
3. I look at tests as opportunities.   *1 2 3 4 5*
4. I read the entire test before answering a question.   *1 2 3 4 5*
5. I know how to answer an essay question.   *1 2 3 4 5*
6. I know what qualifiers make a statement true or false.   *1 2 3 4 5*
7. I agree that it is important to learn thoroughly.   *1 2 3 4 5*
8. I know the type of test I like best.   *1 2 3 4 5*
9. I enjoy multiple-choice tests.   *1 2 3 4 5*
10. I enjoy essay tests.   *1 2 3 4 5*

5=Strongly Agree
4=Agree
3=Don't Know
2=Disagree
1=Strongly Disagree

TOTAL YOUR POINTS from these ten questions. Refer to the following rating scale to determine how good you are at taking tests.

0–10   Your test-taking skills are poor.
11–20 Your test-taking skills are below average.
21–30 Your test-taking skills are average.
31–40 Your test-taking skills are above average.
41–50 Your test-taking skills are excellent.

Does your score and the rating scale match what you feel about your test-taking abilities? If not, don't worry. If you read this chapter carefully and complete the exercises within, your test-taking skills will be enhanced.

Why Do I Have to Take a Test?

Do you enjoy taking tests? Most students don't. Many dread it and believe that teachers are trying to make their lives miserable. This attitude can defeat you. You need to view tests as an opportunity to show how much you know about a skill or subject. Tests should be viewed as a challenge that can help you to learn and grow.

Tests are designed to measure how well you have mastered a skill or concept. In addition, taking a test is another opportunity for you to learn new information. Tests are a fact of life, and they are everywhere. The driver's test, SATI, employee evaluations, eye exams, and blood tests are types of tests. The list could be practically endless.

Doing your best on a test can mean passing a course, earning a degree, or being promoted at work. Therefore, it is important that you accept test taking as a fact of life. If you prepare appropriately and have confidence, your chance for experiencing success is greatly enhanced. List the reasons why you believe your instructors give tests.

1. _____
2. _____
3. _____
4. _____
5. _____

Your list may include the following reasons: to make my life miserable, to motivate me to learn and study, to show me what I don't know or understand, to show the teacher what needs to be re-taught, to determine my grade in a course, and to teach information.

Controlling Test Anxiety

OK, so test anxiety is a natural response. You maybe nervous prior to taking a test because you want to do well on it. Anxiety is created because you fear that you may not do as well as you had hoped. Believe it or not, some anxiety can actually increase your success, because you are more aware, atuned, and physically alert.

However, there are reasons other than the fear of failure for why you may be anxious during a test. List the reasons why you think students become anxious during tests:

1. _____
2. _____
3. _____
4. _____

Perhaps your list includes such reasons as studying the wrong material, failing to study, failing to understand the information, getting nervous when taking a test, being unable to concentrate, experiencing distractions in the room, forgetting to take needed materials to the test, and being unsure of the test day.

Which reasons in your list can be controlled? _____
_____
_____
_____
_____

Test anxiety can cause frustration, but relax; a great deal of it is controllable. Test anxiety can be dramatically reduced when you are in control of the testing situation. By studying and thoroughly learning the material, by using test-taking strategies, and by entering the test with confidence, you can gain the measure of control that you need. As long as you give 100% (your very best), the outcome will be positive. It is important to realize that we all have limitations and academic weaknesses. None of us is good at everything. You will need to identify and focus on your strengths and not let your weaknesses hold you back.

When do you experience test anxiety? _____
_____
_____
_____

What could you do to control your anxiety? _____
_____
_____
_____

ROADWAYS TO REDUCING TEST ANXIETY

- Thoroughly learn the material.
- Approach the test with a positive attitude.
- Chewing gum or eating hard candy helps relax some students.
- Take a break from the test.
- Get a good night's sleep the night before.
- Eat a healthy meal before the test.
- Arrive twenty minutes early.
- Take deep breaths if you find yourself becoming nervous.
- Enter the test with all materials needed for the test.
- Reward yourself for a job well done.

Preparing for Tests

Test anxiety is a fact of life for most students. Learning to cope with this anxiety is a step in the right direction.

Understanding the different types of test questions and having strategies for dealing with the types can help you reduce test anxiety.

Students prepare for tests in many different ways. The following are examples of how three different students (The Dreamer, The Procrastinator, and The Planner) prepare for a test:

THE DREAMER

The dreamer is the student who fantasizes or dreams about why he or she might not have to take a test. The night before the exam, this student hopes for some type of national disaster, such as a snowstorm or flood, to close school. Or, this student hopes that the instructor will be sick and class will be cancelled. Most of these students will fail the test or just squeak by.

THE PROCRASTINATOR

The procrastinator is the student who puts off studying for the test until the night before. This student will stay up all night cramming as much information as possible into his or her brain. Some of the procrastinators will manage to make a C on the test, and a few of the procrastinators, who do their best work under pressure, will manage to make better than a C.

THE PLANNER

The planner is the student who prepares for the exam. This student spends several days, even weeks, preparing for the exam. This student reviews reading assignments, notes, and handouts. The planner will create a mock test consisting of questions he or she feels might be asked on the test. These students tend to be more confident and experience less test anxiety. They have learned that there is no substitute for studying and planning for a test. The planner is able to do his or her best on the exam and usually makes the best grades.

Which student best describes you? _____

Why? _____

_____

_____

_____

_____

_____

ROADWAYS TO PREPARING FOR A TEST

- Create a study schedule as soon as a test is scheduled.
- Ask your instructor what information will be tested.
- Find out how you will be tested, for example, essay or multiple choice.
- Write a list of questions you think might be asked on the test.
- Form a study group with which to study several days prior to the test.
- Make a list of questions from notes and reading assignments that still don't make sense, and ask the instructor for additional clarification.
- Above all, get a good night's sleep the night before the test, and eat a healthy meal before the test.

Test-Taking Strategies

Instructors present information in a variety of ways, and the way they ask questions on tests also varies. When you spend time preparing for a test, you want to do well. You can accomplish this by understanding the different kinds of test questions and knowing the best way to answer them. Most students prefer certain types of questions more than others. You may prefer multiple-choice questions, for example, over essay questions. Regardless of what you prefer, you should be familiar with all kinds of questions and know how to best answer them. The most common kinds of test questions are:

Matching questions

True/false questions

Multiple-choice questions

Short-answer questions

Essay questions

In addition to knowing the kinds of test questions, it is also helpful to know general test-taking techniques and specific strategies for answering each kind of question. The information in this section will help you take tests and answer different kinds of questions. However, relying on the strategies alone will not help you. As previously mentioned (several times), thoroughly learning the material is the best test-taking tool. It reduces anxiety and builds confidence. Being prepared means you will do well on the test.

General Test-Taking Techniques

1. Read and follow all directions.

2. Answer the easiest questions first.

3. Watch the time limits.

4. Read the questions carefully.

5. Answer every question, if there is no penalty for guessing.

6. Ask for clarification, if permitted.

7. Skim through the entire test before beginning.

8. Watch for words that may change the meaning of the sentence, such as *not, either/or, always*, and so forth.

9. Answer the questions neatly.

10. Above all, *think positively*!

These general test-taking techniques apply to all kinds of tests. The use of these techniques can increase your academic success. In the following sections, you will be given explanations and simple examples of the various types of test questions.

Strategies for Answering Matching Questions

Matching questions often test your understanding of people, places, things, dates, and vocabulary. The objective when answering matching questions is to match information in two columns. Strategies for answering matching questions are outlined in the following list:

1. First, read through each column.

2. Match the easiest information first.

3. Lightly cross out information as it is matched.

4. Use a process of elimination to match difficult or unknown information.

5. Leave *no* questions blank, if there is no penalty for guessing.

Directions: Match the terms in column A with the characteristics in column B.

	A		B
1.	Listening	a.	Open-minded
2.	Objectively	b.	Prejudging
3.	Obstacle	c.	Automatic

Strategies for Answering True/False Questions

In a true/false question, you determine whether or not a statement is correct. Strategies for answering true/false questions are revealed in the following list:

1. Read the statement carefully.

2. Pay attention to special words that may indicate that the statement is true—words such as *some, few, many, often*, and so on.

3. Pay attention to special words that *may* indicate that the statement is false—words such as *never, all, every, only*, and so on.

4. If any part of a statement is false, then the entire statement is considered false.

5. Answer every question, if there is no penalty for guessing.

6. When in doubt, choose *true*.

7. Never try to fake the answer by making the T look like it could be either T or F.

Directions: Write T for *true* or F for *false*.

_____ 1. *System-imposed time can always be controlled.*

_____ 2. *Everyone has the same amount of time.*

_____ 3. *Prioritizing is a technique that lets you know what is most important.*

Strategies for Answering Multiple-Choice Questions

Multiple-choice questions are common test questions. In fact, most standardized tests use this format. When answering multiple-choice test questions, you must answer a question or complete a statement by selecting the correct answer from two, three, four, or five possible answer choices. Strategies for answering multiple-choice questions are provided in the following list:

1. Carefully read the statement and try to answer the question before you read the answer choices.

2. Answers containing words such as *never, all, every, best, worst*, and *only* can usually be eliminated as an answer choice.

3. Lightly cross out answers that you feel or know are incorrect.

4. Read all the options before making your decision.

5. If the answers are dates or numbers, you can usually rule out the lowest and highest answer.

6. Answer each question, if there is no penalty for guessing.

   Directions: Read each statement and circle the correct answer.

1. Which is not a step in the listening process?

   a. Receiving

   b. Reacting

   c. Organizing

   d. Accepting

2. Which is not a tip for increasing self-esteem?

   a. Embrace the notion: I am responsible for my own life.

   b. Compare yourself with others.

   c. Control your self-talk.

   d. Take at least one positive risk a week.

3. Which technique should be used when studying a chapter in a textbook?

   a. ROAR

   b. DADE

   c. SQ3R

   d. L-STAR

Strategies for Answering Short-Answer Questions

Tests that include short-answer or fill-in-the-blank questions ask you to supply the information. Short-answer questions will not provide answer choices; therefore, you must depend on the information you have stored in your long-term memory. Strategies for answering short-answer or fill-in-the-blank questions are the following:

1. Read the question carefully to make certain you understand how to answer it.

2. Be short and to the point.

3. Never leave a blank unless there is a penalty for guessing. Write something; a few points are better than none.

4. Look for answers or clues to the questions in the test itself.

Directions: Answer each question/statement by filling in the blank or writing a complete sentence.

1. Name four of the five types of mnemonic devices. _____
_____

2. One of the best ways to study a textbook is to use the SQ3R method. What does SQ3R stand for? _____
_____
_____

3. A technique used to decode an unfamiliar word by examining parts of the word is known as _____.

Strategies for Answering Essay Questions

An essay question gives you an opportunity to share what you know. Like the short-answer question, the essay question also requires that you supply the entire answer from memory. Answering essay questions can be difficult if you lack certain skills. Being able to write well and to think clearly are two skills that you will surely need. Writing well includes the ability to choose precise words, to punctuate correctly, and to organize your ideas. If you want to do well at answering essay questions, you will need to understand what an essay question is asking and to think clearly in organizing your answers. Many essay questions will ask you either to explain, to compare, to contrast, or to define an event or idea. When you are asked *to explain* an event or idea, the instructor will be asking you to give reasons why an event took place or to offer a description of an idea. In fact, an instructor might ask you to explain the events leading up to a particular incident. In this case, you would most likely provide the events in a time sequence (what happened first, what happened next, and what happened last).

> **Example:** Explain why you would rather travel on a small, two-lane highway than on a giant freeway.
>
> *There are a number of reasons why I would prefer to travel on a two-lane highway than on a freeway. First, two-lane highways take you to places where freeways are unwelcome. Two-lane roads, for instance, can take you to small towns, through national forests, and to remote areas with much beautiful scenery. Second, I enjoy traveling on two-lane highways because of the terrible traffic on giant freeways. When traveling on two-lane roads, I don't feel like I'm constantly dodging other cars. Finally, on a two-lane road, I can take my time and enjoy the view. I can, for example, travel at my own pace and can stop to look at something that captures my interest.*

If an instructor asked you *to compare* an event or idea with another event or idea, you would tell how the two ideas or events are alike. Similarly, if this same teacher asked you to contrast two events or ideas, you would show how they are different. An instructor will sometimes ask you to compare and to contrast at the same time. In this case, you simply tell how two events or ideas are alike and how they are different. (Using a paragraph for similarities and a paragraph for differences is a good idea).

> **Example:** Compare and contrast a freeway and a two-lane road (sometimes called a country road).
>
> *Freeways and two-lane roads are alike in at least two ways. First, they are both pathways designed to take you to some other place. Second, they are alike in the materials used in their construction. Concrete and asphalt, for instance, are used to construct both freeways and two-lane roads.*
> *Although, they are similar in at least two ways, freeways and two-lane roads share many differences. Freeways take up much more space (because of the numerous lanes of traffic) than do two-lane roads. Unlike two-lane roads, freeways also fail to run through many picturesque small towns.*

When you are asked *to define* a term, you are being asked to provide information about what a term means. A definition should include placing the thing to be defined into a class of similar things and then telling how it is different from all the other things in the class.

Example: Define the term *freeway*.

A freeway is a type of highway that has many lanes of traffic. The traffic is sometimes going in only one direction; but in most cases, there are numerous lanes of traffic going in both directions.

Explanation: The freeway is put in a class (highways). The definition also tells how the freeway is different from other highways (many lanes of traffic).

Strategies for answering essay questions:

1. When reading the questions, pay particular attention to the special words, such as *explain, compare and contrast,* or *define*. Make sure you are answering the question correctly.

2. Make an outline to organize your thoughts.

3. Be neat.

4. Be careful with grammar, spelling, and punctuation.

5. Mention details (names, dates, events).

6. Write a strong introduction and conclusion.

7. Do not write meaningless information just to fill the page. (Instructors can't stand it.)

Directions: Answer the following essay question, using complete and coherent sentences.

Explain why it is important to have a good education. _____

_____

_____

_____

_____

Observations

Tests do not have to be dreaded. Your instructors are not trying to punish you. Tests are an opportunity for you to show how much you have learned and to impress your instructors and yourself with your knowledge. The grades that you earn will reflect the amount of energy you put into studying. Take control by attending class, taking notes, asking questions, completing assignments, and over-learning material. Striving to always do your best will pay off in the end.

As a Result of this Chapter, and in Preparing for My Journey, I Plan to . . .

CHAPTER 9

Stopping to Ask for Directions
Campus Resources

Chapter 9

> The real object of education is to give students resources that will endure as long as life endures; habits that time will not destroy; occupations that will render sickness tolerable, solitude pleasant, life more dignified and useful, and death less terrible.
>
> *Sidney Smith, educator*

Leí was nearing the completion of her second semester in college. She had done quite well academically but one problem remained—Leí did not know what she wanted to do for her life's work. She had struggled with the question since the ninth grade. She had thought about being an artist, an engineer, or a designer. When it was time to register for her third semester of classes, Leí realized that she should make a decision before a lot of time and money would be lost by taking courses that she would not need.

At that time, her advisor suggested that she visit the college career center and schedule an appointment with a counselor in that area. Her advisor suggested that she have a career assessment that would point out her strengths and suggest careers that maybe Leí had not thought of before. During the appointment with the counselor, Leí was able to complete various inventories that assisted her with making a decision about her career. Leí completed the Myers-Briggs Personality Type Indicator, the Strong Interest Inventory, and some local inventories that had been developed by her campus. She was also able to work on the computer and used the College Board's SIGI program to further analyze her interests.

Armed with this information, Leí went to the library and researched several careers. As a result of using these campus resources, Leí is planning to pursue her new dream of becoming an engineer and will take her first courses related to this major in the Fall.

The Importance of Resources

This chapter is designed to help you understand what resources are typically available on a college campus. Colleges vary in the type of resources and services they offer to students based on where they are located, the kind of student that they serve, and whether the campus has commuter or residential students. At the end of this chapter, you should be able to

- Identify tangible and intangible resources
- Understand what resources are typically available on most college campuses
- Discuss campus resources, such as the library, computer labs, and special needs labs (writing, math, reading, etc.)
- Use resources available on your campus

Before you begin this chapter, take a few moments and answer the following questions. These questions are designed to determine what you already know about what your college offers.

SELF-STUDY

5=Strongly Agree
4=Agree
3=Don't Know
2=Disagree
1=Strongly Disagree

1. I know how to use the college catalog.
   1 2 3 4 5

2. I know how to find the college library.
   1 2 3 4 5

3. I know where to find services that I need, such as financial aid, job placement, counseling, and so on.
   1 2 3 4 5

4. I am aware of the computer options available to me on the campus.
   1 2 3 4 5

5. I know my academic advisor.
   1 2 3 4 5

6. I know where to go to get help with my classes.
   1 2 3 4 5

7. I am aware of various campus organizations and clubs.
   1 2 3 4 5

8. I understand the student handbook.
   1 2 3 4 5

9. I am aware of counseling services available to me on campus.
   1 2 3 4 5

10. I understand the college withdrawal/drop policy.
    1 2 3 4 5

TOTAL YOUR POINTS from these ten questions. Refer to the following rating scale to determine where you stand in relation to dealing with career decisions.

0–10 You probably are not aware of any of the services available to you on your campus; continue to read on—you have much to learn about what is available to you.

11–20 You probably have some knowledge of services and resources that are available, but you may not know where to find the resources you need or when to use them.

21–30 You may have used some of the services available to you on campus.

31–40 You have probably used some of the services on campus and utilized some of the resources; you could learn more to get the most from your college education.

41–50 You, no doubt, have become quite proficient with learning what is available on your campus; read on, however—there is much more to learn as you begin your educational journey.

Tangible Versus Intangible Resources

Before a discussion of resources, some discussion about tangible resources versus intangible resources needs to be addressed. Tangible resources are things you can see, feel, taste, hear, or smell. Tangible resources are "real" things—things such as money for college, books with which to learn, computers to use for producing papers, and so forth. Intangible resources, on the other hand, cannot necessarily be touched or seen. In a college setting, intangible resources are resources that are in place to support your overall education. These resources take the shape of "services" and include things such as tutoring, counseling, and help with academic subjects or advice from your professors. All resources, both tangible and intangible, are important, and all play a major role in helping you become a successful student.

In the space provided, list some tangible and intangible resources that you are aware of on your campus.

Tangible Resources	Intangible Resources

What sort of tangible resources did you list? Did you include computers? The library? Maybe even the college catalog? Maybe the health center? Under intangible resources, were you able to also mention advisors, counselors, and student organizations? All of these resources serve to form a network of services on your campus. This chapter is designed to explain in further detail some of these resources and to direct you to others on your campus.

The Owner's Manual: Your College Catalog

When you buy a new car, you usually can depend on having an owner's manual included with the purchase. The owner's manual helps you understand every aspect of your new car—from how to check the oil to how to dim the lights. All aspects of owning your new car are covered in this one little book. Just as you would have received an owner's manual when you purchased a new car, you should also have received a college catalog when you were accepted to your institution.

Some colleges will provide you with a college catalog before you register for courses, but all colleges are obligated to provide you with a catalog once you enroll. This college catalog is an owner's manual for your time in college—hang on to this catalog and consult it often. It is important that you keep this document as you move through your educational experience. Many requirements may change as you are enrolled; colleges will typically "grandfather" students already enrolled. That is to say, if requirements change, you will not typically be required to meet the new requirements—you will be bound by the requirements that were in effect at the time you entered. Your college catalog should offer answers to questions such as, "What are the graduation requirements for this institution?" "What do I have to make to be able to be on the Dean's List?" "What are the courses required in my major in order for me to graduate?" In addition to these answers, other questions you have about your college experience will also be answered in this catalog.

A catalog is one resource—a tangible resource that you should use often. Refer to the catalog often to see what is required and what you have left to do in order to graduate. For this next exercise, find your major in your college catalog. Write the name of your major and the degree you will receive, as well as the page number that the course requirements are listed on. For example:

Major: Machine Tool Technology

Degree: Associate of Applied Science

Page: 43

Major: _____

Degree: _____

Page: _____

Review the courses required for you to graduate in your major. How many hours (semester or quarter) will be required for you to graduate? (Hint: Some colleges divide the courses into suggested schedules for each term you are enrolled; often, the hours represented by the courses are added for you.) List the number of hours required to graduate from your program: _____

Doing some simple division, estimate the number of semesters or quarters that will be required for you to complete your degree. Example:

60 semester hours required to complete, 15 hours each semester, 4 semesters or 2 years

_____

_____

This is your projected completion time—the time when you will reasonably expect to graduate. Determining this date will help you put your studies in perspective. Just as you use milestones as you are traveling, knowing where you are in your educational journey will help you keep your final destination (graduation) in focus and help you see the progress that you are making.

Now, take a look at the courses that are required for your particular major; check the catalog to see if these courses have prerequisites. Prerequisites are courses, or requirements, that must be satisfied before you can move on to the content of the course. Do any of your courses have prerequisites? What are some of the prerequisites? List some of the courses with prerequisites and write out what the prerequisites are:

_____
_____
_____
_____
_____
_____
_____

College catalogs are wonderful resources for many other questions that may arise. For example, say you want to know the policy on repeating courses; just turn to the index and it will refer you to the page for the answer. Often, college catalogs list professor's complete names and the schools from which they earned their degrees. If nothing else, it is interesting to see where your professors studied. In addition, the college catalog can explain how to become involved in student activities, and can list the hours for the student bookstore, and student union, just to name a few. In short, the college catalog should be your best friend as you go through the process of earning your degree. *Keep the catalog and refer to it often!*

Catalog Scavenger Hunt

1. My college was founded in _____.
2. My college president is _____.
3. My college offers _____ degrees.
4. My Department Chair is _____.
5. The college Mission Statement is on page _____.
6. Information about student records is found on page _____.
7. A map of the campus is on page _____.
8. My college has _____ (number of) campuses.
9. College fees are listed on page _____.
10. The withdrawal/college policy is on page _____.
11. I'm put on academic probation when my GPA falls below _____.
12. The policy for plagiarism is found on page _____.

Knowing where to find particular items in the catalog is important—the catalog is the road map of your educational journey and being able to read a map is important (especially if you get lost). Spend some time getting to know your catalog. You'll be glad that you did when you need to find important information in a hurry.

The Library

If the classroom is the heartbeat of the college, the library is the brain. The library is a wonderful resource that will enable you to get the most out of your educational journey. The library is one place on campus that houses numerous resources—usually under one roof. In the library, you will find books, magazines or journals (referred to as periodicals), tapes (both audio and video), maps, government documents, microfilm, microfiche, CDs, and computers that will link you to the information highway. (More about the highway later.)

The library is best used as a daily tool, whether as a quiet place to study or as a place in which to "get directions" and find out more about "points of interest" throughout your journey. The library can make you feel uncomfortable, too—that is, until you learn to use it properly.

Most libraries have some sort of tour that will help you become acquainted with what is available. Take the time to take the library tour. You will never be sorry that you did! If you are still unclear about where a particular item is located or how to use a special piece of equipment, ask! Librarians earn their living by giving out information. Most are happy to help you at any time. Librarians won't do your work for you, however. The librarian is also a resource. Use the librarian's knowledge and time wisely. The library tour will also help you to determine which cataloging system the library is using—Dewey Decimal (DD) or Library of Congress (LC). A cataloging system is simply a way in which libraries group similar books together. Don't let this make you feel uncomfortable. The system is easily learned and, again, if you get "stuck," a librarian is always ready to help.

Library Scavenger Hunt

1. Who wrote Gone With The Wind? _____

2. Find an article on computers. _____

3. Locate a book dealing with human behavior. _____

4. For how long can you check out a book? _____

5. The overdue fee is _____

6. The head librarian's name is _____

7. The first line of Shakespeare's *Hamlet* is _____

8. The call number for the *Dictionary of Occupational Titles* is _____
_____

9. Carl Sandburg won a Pulitzer Prize for _____
_____

10. What was the lead story in a newspaper on the date of your birth? ___
_____

Computer Resources: A Trip Along the Information Superhighway

Nearly all colleges and universities are required to include computer literacy as part of the program of study they offer students. No doubt, you will be required to take a course that either deals with computer concepts or computer applications. The definition of a well-rounded student includes computer literacy. You should prepare yourself while you are in college—*computers are now a way of life.*

Computers are such a way of life that many of the services you will need to access while you are in college are delivered through some form of computer application. Some colleges and universities offer Internet services (a link to worldwide information) to their students; take advantage of this service if it is offered to you.

There is so much to learn on the Internet and you can have a tremendous amount of fun as well. Cyberspace can open up new worlds for you. You will be able to access information that you never knew existed. Apart from being able to find valuable information, "surfing the net" is fun, entertaining, and educational! Who knows, you may even meet someone in Australia or Europe over the Internet. Many people who have a special hobby are able to "talk" to others with similar interests.

Computers can also help you to be a better student. Today, there are software packages that will help you with your math, your writing, and your grammar. Some computer programs make learning seem like a game—a game that is fun as well as educational. Check with your library or tutoring center to see what software packages are available to help you with various subjects. Your academic advisor can also direct you to resources on campus that are related to learning while using computers.

Computers are such a way of life that you will not be able to escape using one before you graduate. You should learn to feel comfortable with computers and remember that they are a tool—a tool to help you be a successful student.

Making a Pit Stop: Learning Resource Centers

Occasionally, your academic journey can be a little bumpy. Maybe you turned in a paper and did not receive the grade that you had expected. Maybe you took a math test and didn't do as well as you had hoped. Don't despair! On most campuses, help is available in learning centers often referred to as "The Math Center," "The Reading Center," or "The Writing Center." If these services are available on your campus, you should take advantage of the help that they can provide.

These centers employ students as well as professional tutors who can help you through your academic problems. Often, these centers also have video or audio tapes that can help with specific problems. Help is available in one form or another. For instance, if you are having a problem with fractions, someone from the math center can show you how to add, subtract, multiply, or divide fractions, and maybe go through your homework or your class assignments and then show you a videotape that will discuss fractions. The same would be true if you were having problems with adverbs; help would be available in the writing center. Often, these centers can give you practice work and let you work on specific academic problems you may be having while you are in the center. This is one resource of which you definitely will want to take advantage. Use these centers to your advantage and benefit. You can only be a better student in the long run by utilizing these services.

The Math Center phone number is _____.

CAMPUS RESOURCES

The Math Center is located in _____.

The Reading Center phone number is _____.

The Reading Center is located in _____.

The Writing Center phone number is _____.

The Writing Center is located in _____.

Traveling Companions: Your Friends

A discussion about resources is not complete without mentioning one of the most valuable resources, your friends. Friends can make your journey easier, help you understand difficult material, and even quiz you before an exam. Friends can help you through the rocky roads you may encounter along the way and can help make your journey more enjoyable. A supportive friend can keep you going when you feel like giving up and can help you understand your options.

Friends are valuable resources, but they can also be your biggest problem. When choosing friends, choose carefully. If a friend is causing you to get behind in your schoolwork because you are constantly being encouraged to do other things and be involved with activities that keep you from studying, think about whether you want to be a friend with that particular person. Don't let someone else rob you of your chance to be a more educated person; again, choose your friends wisely.

Counseling Services

There are times in almost everyone's life when they might need a little help dealing with a variety of different problems. Sometimes, we just need to talk to someone who can look at our situation with an open mind and help us work toward solutions and answers. On the college campus, these services can be in the form of emotional counseling services or career counseling services. Usually, your college will have trained professionals in each area to help you make healthy decisions regarding your problems. An extensive discussion of career counseling is located in Chapter 11.

One of the most important things to remember is that if you are in need of counseling—career, academic, or emotional—the best advice is to seek out someone on campus with whom you feel comfortable and talk with her. It probably isn't a wise decision to let the situation grow and fester. These services are free to you and may make your days as a freshman easier. Some students feel embarrassed or ashamed to have to seek counseling, but the fact is that many, many students need and seek advice—from money problems to relationship break-ups—everyday. Asking for advice and help is a wise decision for many students.

Financial Aid Services

Even the best laid plans are sometimes cut short by financial problems. It is usually understood that college students are not rich and have to do a variety of jobs and apply for an array of scholarships and aid to make it through college. Many students wait until it is too late to seek financial counseling and apply for financial aid. Logically, you have found the money to be in college or you would not be taking this course.

CAMPUS RESOURCES

However, it may be that you see that your funds are running low, and you may have to stop out of college for a year or a semester. Wait! Before you make that decision, talk to a financial aid counselor. They are trained in the art of helping students find scholarships; federal, state, and local aid; and jobs for college students. Stopping out may be the first thing on your mind, but it may be a last resort if you plan ahead and seek financial aid advice early.

The most obvious type of financial assistance is federal and state financial aid. These programs have been in place for many years, and they are the staple of assistance to many college students. The types of aid available from the federal government are

- Federal Pell grants
- Federal direct loans
- Federal family education loans (FFEL)
- Federal supplemental educational opportunity grants (FSEOG)
- Federal work study (FWS)
- Federal Perkins loans

Not every school takes part in every federal assistance program. To determine which type of aid is available at your school, you should contact the financial aid office.

Some students may be confused about the difference between loans, grants, and work study. According to The Student Guide, published by the Department of Education, the definitions are

- *Grants:* Monies that you don't have to repay
- *Work Study:* Money earned for work that you do at the college. This money does not have to be repaid.
- *Loans:* Borrowed money that you must repay, with interest

As an undergraduate, you may receive all three types of assistance, whereas graduate students cannot receive Pell grants or FSEOGs.

STUDENT ELIGIBILITY FOR FEDERAL FINANCIAL AID

To receive aid from the major student aid programs mentioned, you must

- Have financial need, except for some loan programs
- Have a high school diploma or GED or pass an independently administered test approved by the US Department of Education or meet the standards established by your state

- Be enrolled as a regular student working toward a degree or certificate in an eligible program. You may not receive aid for correspondence or telecommunications courses unless they are a part of an associate, bachelor, or graduate degree program

- Be a U.S. citizen

- Have a valid social security number

- Make satisfactory academic progress

- Sign a statement of educational purpose

- Sign a statement of updated information

- Register with the selective service, if required

(From *The Student Guide*, U.S. Department of Education)

One of the biggest mistake students make when thinking about financial aid is forgetting about scholarships from private industry and social or civic organizations. Each year, millions of dollars are not claimed because students simply did not know about the scholarship or where to find the information. Several resources are available that are worth their weight in millions, simply by researching and applying. To find out more about all types of financial aid, examine the following publications:

Free Dollars from the Federal Government, published by Prentice Hall

Winning Scholarships for College, published by Henry Holt and Company

How to Obtain Maximum Financial Aid, published by Login Publications Consortium

Peterson's 4 Year Colleges, published by Peterson's

Free Money for College, published by Facts on File

Paying for College, published by Villard Books

Financial Aid for College, published by Peterson's

Paying Less for College, published by Peterson's

College Costs and Financial Aid Handbook, published by The College Board

Winning Money for College, published by Peterson's

Free Money for Athletic Scholarships, published by Henry Holt and Company

Don't Miss Out, published by Octameron Press

You will also want to research the following:

Your college catalog (for scholarships at the college)

Your place of employment

Your parent's or spouse's place of employment

Social and civic groups within your community or hometown

Roadways to Applying for Financial Aid

- **Do not miss a deadline. There are *no* exceptions for making up deadlines for federal financial aid!**
- *Read* **all instructions before beginning the process.**
- **Always fill out the application completely and have someone proof your work.**
- **If documentation is required, submit it according to the instructions. Do not fail to do all that the application asks you to do.**
- *Never lie* **about your financial status. This could cost you dearly in the long run.**
- **Begin the application process as soon as possible. *Do not* wait until the last moment. Some aid is given on a first-come, first-served basis. Income tax preparation time is usually financial aid application time.**
- **Talk to the financial aid officer at the institution where you will attend. Person-to-person contact is always best. Never assume anything until you get it in writing.**
- **Take copies of flyers and brochures that are available in the Financial Aid office. Many times, private companies and civic groups will notify the Financial Aid office if they have funds available.**
- **Always apply for admission as well as financial aid. Many awards are given *by* the college to students who are already accepted.**

- **If you are running late with the application, call and ask if there are electronic means to apply.**

- **Always keep a copy of your tax returns for *each* year!**

- **To receive almost *any* money, including some scholarships, you *must* fill out the Free Application for Federal Student Aid form.**

- **Apply for everything possible.**

Health Services

Most college campuses have some type of health or physical services. It is important to know where these facilities are located and what services are available to you. Some colleges included the cost of minor medical care in with tuition. Other colleges offer students a health insurance policy for a very nominal fee. The health services on most campus vary drastically. One college may only have a person who can assist you in finding outside help, while other colleges hire and maintain doctors and nurses for your medical needs. In the space provided, determine what type of health services are available to you on your campus.

The Health Service office is located at _____.

The phone number is _____.

What type of insurance plan does your college offer? _____

What is the price of this insurance? _____

The Next Step

Now that you have become more aware of the tangible and intangible resources available on college campuses, it is time for you to do an inventory of what is available on your college campus. An inventory is simply a listing. Make a list of all of the resources available on *your* college campus. Your college catalog will assist you in being able to complete this exercise.

RESOURCES AVAILABLE TO ME

Academic: _____
_____
_____

Financial: _____
_____
_____

Social: _____
_____
_____

Physical: _____
_____
_____

Career: _____
_____
_____

Religious: _____
_____
_____

Observations

Students who utilize campus resources are more likely to be successful academically, stay involved in the process, make more friends, and stay until graduation than students who do not. You are now aware of what is available on your campus, and you should resolve to take advantage of these services.

I plan to use the following resources before the end of the academic term:

_____
_____
_____
_____
_____
_____
_____
_____
_____
_____
_____
_____
_____
_____
_____
_____
_____
_____
_____
_____
_____
_____
_____

As a Result of this Chapter, and in Preparing for My Journey, I Plan to . . .

CHAPTER 10

Enjoying the Journey
Understanding the Professorate

CHAPTER 10

To teach is to learn twice.
Joseph Joubert

As a young freshman, J.C. was amazed that his professors would actually give him their home phone number. He could not imagine that he would ever need, or want, to call a professor at home about any assignment. J.C. was intrigued by the life of a professor—what did the professor do when he or she was not teaching? Added to that was the "total confusion" about what to call a professor—some were Dr.s, others were not. Some students even referred to the teacher as "Professor Smith." How was he to address this person? How was he to know who this person really was and how he could go about getting help? Compared to high school, this was a different world.

All of these questions added to J.C.'s feelings of being homesick and made him wonder why he was even enrolled in college. This was a new world—a world that he knew very little, if anything, about. It was a world in which the teachers were very different, and no one had told J.C. what to expect or how to react.

My name is James C. Williamson, one of the co-authors of your book. The experience you just read about was my experience as a new freshman in college. As a college student, you may feel that you have entered a new world—a world full of new language, rules, opportunity, and history. This new world can be very scary, can't it? Your success within this new world could depend not only on how well you study, but also on how well you learn the new rules and appreciate the history behind the education you will receive.

This chapter is devoted to helping you understand your professor and make some sense of this new world that you have entered. Have you given much thought to the idea of what a professor's life is like? This chapter is intended to assist you in learning more about the life of a professor and how you can relate to this important person in your education. When you complete this chapter, you should be able to

- Describe the difference between a high school teacher and a college professor
- Understand more about the life of a professor
- Understand the concept of academic freedom and what that concept means to you as a student
- Understand what makes a good student
- Understand what makes a good professor

- Understand some basic classroom etiquette

Following are ten questions that are designed to see what you know about higher education and the differences between your high school teachers and your college professors. Try to spend some time and think about each statement carefully.

SELF-STUDY

5=Strongly Agree
4=Agree
3=Don't Know
2=Disagree
1=Strongly Disagree

1. I understand academic freedom. *1 2 3 4 5*
2. I know how to find my professor's office. *1 2 3 4 5*
3. I know how to approach my professors in their offices. *1 2 3 4 5*
4. I know all of my professors' office hours. *1 2 3 4 5*
5. I know which building my professor's office is located in. *1 2 3 4 5*
6. I understand why my professors have deadlines. *1 2 3 4 5*
7. I know what makes a good student. *1 2 3 4 5*
8. I know how to address my professor. *1 2 3 4 5*
9. I come to class early or stay late if I have questions. *1 2 3 4 5*
10. I know what makes a good professor. *1 2 3 4 5*

TOTAL YOUR POINTS from these ten questions. Refer to the following rating scale to determine where you stand in relation to dealing with the college professorate.

0–10 You probably don't understand any of the major differences between a college professor and a high school teacher. Don't despair. Read on and you will learn a great deal from this chapter.

11–20 You may understand a little about the life of a college professor, but you have much more to learn.

21–30 You have a basic knowledge of what to expect from your professors.

31–40 You have a fairly good idea of what a college professor does and how a professor's life differs from a high school teacher's life.

41–50 You have an excellent grasp of what the professorate is all about. Read on, however, as there are probably aspects of college that you don't yet fully understand.

If you did well on this self-study, you may be well on the way to becoming a better student. At least you understand more about your professors and about college than most students. If most of your score was low, don't despair. This chapter is designed to help you get familiar with the "road" so that your journey will be easier and more worthwhile.

High School Teachers Versus College Professors: What's the Difference?

Historically, higher education, or college, was once reserved only for the "elite" or the very rich and for the training of ministers and preachers. Modern American higher education, on the other hand, is designed "for the people." Because some colleges are designed for the people, community and junior colleges grew across the nation with an open-door policy. An open-door policy basically means that anyone can come to one of these institutions to receive an education regardless of prior academic preparation. There is still a place in higher education for institutions that are selective in their admission of students, and there are a number of college and universities that accept students who are average and below average. In short, this is the beauty of American higher education; there is a place for everyone.

All of these institutions have one thing in common; the instruction that is given is based on hundreds of years of tradition. This tradition dictates what an instructor is called, how an instructor is paid or promoted, and protects "knowledge for knowledge sake" as it is given from instructor to student.

As you begin to read about differences between high school teachers and college professors, it might be wise to write down what you think some of the major differences are. In the space provided, take a few minutes to list some of the differences between high school teachers and college professors:

High School Teachers   **College Professors**

1. _____   1. _____
2. _____   2. _____
3. _____   3. _____
4. _____   4. _____

Who was your favorite high school teacher? _____

_____

What did you like about this teacher? _____

_____

_____

Who is your favorite college professor? _____

_____

What is it about your favorite college professor that you like most? _____

_____

Now, take a minute to look back over your list. Are there lots of differences that you can identify? The way a high school teacher teaches and the way a college professor teaches can be as different as night and day.

Instruction in a college or university is quite different from instruction in a high school. High schools and colleges differ in the approach and philosophy regarding how students should learn. High schools assume much of the responsibility for the students' learning; the teacher is giving the knowledge and facts, and the student is the receiver of this information. Many times, a high school teacher is given a curriculum (or set of goals and information) and then told to teach what is there. A high school teacher usually does not have much input when it comes to the kind of textbook used in the classroom or the content that will be taught.

High school teachers are often evaluated on their job performance by how well students do on standardized tests that have been created to measure how much a student has learned (e.g., BSAP, SATI, etc.). While this approach may be changing in some parts of the country, a high school teacher is usually evaluated on how well a certain group of students did and whether they were promoted to the next level or graduated.

College professors, on the other hand, are evaluated not only on their teaching, but also in other areas. Service such as hospital volunteer work, speaking to groups, research, and scholarship (to include publishing books and articles) are combined to form an evaluation of the instructor. Because of this, a college professor is not only interested in teaching, but also in publishing and public service. Because of this, you may even see your professor's name on the book that you are using or see an article published by him or her.

College professors also value "academic freedom." This term will be discussed a little later on, but basically it means that the details and information of the course are left up to the professor. The professor and his or her department decides how the material will be presented, what book will be used, and how the material will be evaluated. As long as certain topics are covered, the professor has a great deal of freedom in how to structure the course.

Why We Teach in a College

College professors have very special reasons for teaching in a college. Many professors say the chance to be creative in the way they teach and the discussions that students and professors have in class contribute to why they choose to teach on this level. College professors are much more than givers of knowledge; they help to foster stimulating conversation. College professors were surveyed and gave some of the following reasons for teaching in a college as opposed to a high school:

- Not as many discipline problems in a college
- "Feels" more like a profession
- Likes the fact that students are responsible for their own learning
- Freedom to teach controversial subjects
- Students seem more "ready" to learn

The Life of a Professor

Although it may seem that your professor's life is one of leisure and lots of free time, the opposite is true. For professors to keep up with what is happening in their fields, they must *constantly* read, study, and learn about the latest developments. A professor spends a great deal of time reading. Committed and dedicated professors are not satisfied with teaching a course the same way time after time. Great professors are always trying to improve what they bring to the student. Because of this, professors spend a great

deal of time doing research for books and courses and publishing articles. Publishing is very important to most professors, and they are very proud of the works they have published. In addition, professors are asked to present their research at conferences and to give workshops and seminars.

In addition to teaching classes, doing research, writing articles and books, and presenting at conferences, a professor's time is also taken up by students. More than likely, you have a professor as an academic advisor. The academic advisor provides academic assistance to you semester after semester. Most advisors have a large number of students that they must see each semester.

Ranking, or seniority, is very important to a professor. Because this is important, the professor will spend many hours trying to become a better teacher or researcher in order to be ranked at a higher level. Generally, ranking follows the order of

- Instructors (beginning professors)
- Instructors then become Assistant Professors
- Assistant Professors become Associate Professors
- Associate Professors become Professors (this step is sometimes referred to as "full" professor)

Although it is not extremely important to know what rank your professor is, this explanation should help you understand what is important to your professor. This discussion should also help you understand the words that you may hear the professor use when he or she talks about rank.

Academic Freedom and What It Means to You

The "right" of the professor to teach controversial subject matter or subject matter that might be viewed as different or uncommon is known as academic freedom. As long as the basic ideas of a course are taught, colleges and universities usually leave the way the course is taught to the professor. The professor decides when exams are given and their format. Professors also decide if they want to lecture most of the time, use classroom exercises to show a point, or have students complete outside assignments. Basically, it allows professors the freedom to approach the subject matter in whatever manner they choose. For the student, it gives the opportunity to experience many different approaches to learning. The student may be asked to write a paper in one class, put together a group presentation in another class, and recite a reading in yet another class.

Another benefit for the student is that the teacher has chosen the approach with which he or she is more comfortable. The student, therefore, is the one who benefits from the fact that the professor feels particularly comfortable with the approach he is using.

Controversial subject matter can be discussed within the framework of academic freedom, and the subject matter is quite different in a college as opposed to a high school. Subjects that normally might be viewed as taboo in high schools can be discussed, debated, and deliberated in college, all because of academic freedom.

Academic freedom makes the United States system of higher education unique; as such, it allows students to experience a wide variety of approaches and tends to make the collegiate experience richer and more rewarding.

Briefly list several different assignments or projects you have had to do this semester:

1. _____
2. _____
3. _____
4. _____

Which assignment did you enjoy the most? _____
_____

Why do you think you enjoyed this particular assignment? _____

_____

_____

Which assignment did you enjoy least? _____

_____

Why do you think you did not enjoy this particular assignment? _____

_____

_____

Examine the teaching style of your favorite professor. What is his or her dominant style? Is it the lecture method? Do you like this style? According to Dunn and Dunn (1993) many teachers use both a left and right brain approach when teaching. This type of teaching is appropriate for all types of learners. Some instructors will present information using only an analytical, or left brain, approach. Their instruction usually includes a lot of teacher explanation and visual aids with specific, detailed directions, and they give tests often. Teachers who use a global, or right brain, approach might introduce a lesson with a joke or short story. This kind of instructor would encourage students to think for themselves and would probably be using group learning or discovery as the basic approach to teaching. The professor that uses this kind of approach may test using presentations, charts, games, and so on. As a student, it is very important that you be able to recognize these differences with certain professors and be able to deal with each style. Just as you have preferences in the way you like to learn, professors have preferences in the way they like to teach. Being a successful student means being able to identify the professor's method or style and then changing your study habits to be successful with that particular method.

Examine the teaching style of one of your current professors. Describe it.

_____

_____

_____

Do you like this particular style? Why or Why not?

_____

_____

_____

Understanding What the Professor Wants

Your professor will give you a syllabus on the first day of class. The syllabus outlines specifically what is expected of you during the course. A syllabus is generally considered a contract that assures you that course requirements cannot be changed in the middle of the term. On the syllabus, you may be able to find out when tests are to be given, what other work will be required for the course (papers, book reviews, etc.) and how much each will count toward your final grade. You will probably also see the attendance policy for your school and the course. Some professors also include important dates during the semester, such as the last day to withdraw, the last day to add, and so forth. What you might not find out by reading the syllabus is what the professor *really* expects of you—does she expect you to "skim" chapters and be familiar with ideas or does she expect you to be specific in your reading? One of the best ways to find out what your professor expects is to ask! Ask her how you should prepare for class each day. The professor will be impressed that you care enough to find out what is expected of you, and you will begin to understand more about what the professor expects. Another helpful hint is to ask other students who have had the professor during a previous term what the professor was like. Find out what the professor expects and how you can adapt your study habits to be successful in the class.

Questions to Ask Other Students about Professors

1. How much outside reading does the professor require?

2. What are the tests like? Are they multiple choice, true-false, or essay?

3. How closely does the professor follow the grading scale?

4. What grade did you make? Why do you feel that you made this grade?

5. What would you change if you had to take the course again?

6. Would you take this professor for another class?

7. Did you learn a lot?

Above all else, ask ask ask! If you do not ask the instructor, or some of your peers, you are dealing with an unknown. This unknown could cost you a grade during the first part of the term, and it may be impossible for you to get caught up later during the term.

What Makes a Good Student

A survey of professors around the nation was administered, and they were asked what makes a good student. They were asked to comment on the biggest differences that they had noticed in students of today. Additionally, they were asked about what they liked most about students of today and what they liked least about students of today. The following answers were given:

- The biggest difference in students of today has to do with the fact that students of today are more opinionated and more verbal.

- Students of today are better prepared academically.

- Students of today are looking at a limited job market, and so therefore, they are more focused—they "know" why they are in school. I also like the diversity that I see today.

Another question asked, "Beyond the information that you give daily, what is the most important message that you want to leave with your students?" One of the best answers given was

- I hope that I can instill in my students the ability to look *beyond* and not simply "accept" that a problem will automatically have an answer that is black or white, right or wrong, good or bad. To see shades of differences and to have empathy is important. I also want my students to be able to deal with change and to *like learning!*

Finally, professors were asked what they thought made a "good" student. The responses are very interesting, and you may want to take a few minutes to read them.

- A "good" student is . . . one who is self-motivated and who wants to do more than just memorize. One who really *wants* to understand and apply concepts.

- A "good" student is . . . a student who has a genuine desire to learn and takes the *time* to learn new information.

- A "good" student is . . . one who wants to learn, explores the boundaries of information, is not passive but is active in gaining knowledge.

- A good student accepts academic responsibility.

To summarize, professors seem to like students who (1) want to learn, (2) are self-motivated, (3) question what they are learning and try to relate it to "real" issues, and (4) have a sense of why they are in school.

What Makes a Good Professor

Just like professors, students were also given a survey and asked to respond to questions. The first question was, "What is the biggest difference between your college professors and your high school instructors?" Student responses were

- College professors require more from you than high school instructors. I like my college professors because they treat you like adults instead of kids.

- College professors go into detail on almost everything; they are very specific and are not easily strayed off of the subject.

- College professors make you think more. High school teachers also gave you a great review and basically told you what would be on the test—college professors don't do that.

The second question asked was, "What do you like most about your college professors?" and the third was, "What do you like least about your college professors?" Student answers were

- What do I like most about college professors? They are *demanding*.

- College professors are passionate about what they teach—they have a real interest in the subject.

Finally, one student, when responding to the question, "What makes an effective college professor?" indicated that

- College professors set higher expectations with little direction, which forces you to become more responsible and devoted to your schoolwork.

In summary, college students expect college professors to be harder, and they are. College professors demand a lot and expect you to be able to keep up the pace when you are in their classes.

Classroom Etiquette

Classroom etiquette, or knowing how to properly conduct yourself in a college setting, is very important as you begin your journey. One of the most important things about being a good student is realizing that you are not the only person in the room. There may be times when you are not interested in what is being said, but the person next to you may need the information. Being a responsible student means having respect for the other people in your class *and* respect for the instructor. The following points, although they may seem "preachy," are designed to help you get more from your college experience. Several ways in which you can respect the instructor and other students:

1. If, for some unforeseen reason, you have to be late for class, you should not make loud noises when you enter the room. Never walk in front of the instructor as you enter the room. If you usually sit on the side of the room, do not worry about your regular seat. Take the seat that is closest to the door.

2. Eating, drinking, or using tobacco products in a classroom setting, unless the professor has given you permission to do so, is rude.

3. If you must leave class early, it is important that you tell the professor before class. If you feel that you have to leave class early once or twice a week, perhaps it is best for all involved if you drop the course or have your counselor arrange for you to take another section.

4. Don't start to pack up your book bag or other materials and begin to rustle through your books and papers before your professor has dismissed class. Few things will make your professor angrier than this situation. Some even refer to this as "book bag levitation."

5. Please don't start a conversation with another student during the lecture, regardless of the subject matter. Even if you missed something the professor said, it is better to stop the professor than to

start a conversation with another student. Use the time before and after class to discuss topics with other students.

6. When visiting a professor's office, you should try to make an appointment instead of just showing up. Many times, the professor may be grading papers, working on school projects, or helping other students. If you must go to the professor without an appointment, never enter the office without knocking. Also, if you did not have an appointment, make your visit quick. Have your questions lined up *before* you knock on the door. Ask if this is a convenient time for you to interrupt.

7. Common courtesy dictates that you will not enter a professor's office without permission, even if the door is open. Always knock and wait to be invited in.

8. If you disagree with a grade that you have received, you should make an appointment to talk with the professor and ask him to go over the specifics of the grade. Approach the conversation from the perspective that you are just trying to understand what you did wrong so that you will learn from your mistakes and not make the same mistake again. Try not to be defensive. Professors like for students to be interested enough in their work to question and probe—just do so diplomatically!

You should extend the same amount of courtesy to your professors and fellow students that you expect. Your journey will be more enjoyable if you pay attention to being nice along the way.

Reading the Professor's Schedule

As you begin to learn where your professor's office is located, you will also notice, should you happen to visit, that most professors will post their schedule outside of their door. Reading a professor's schedule is really very easy. Usually, a professor will post the hours that she is teaching, the hours reserved for office hours, and may include other important information such as lunch and prep time. A typical professor's schedule might look something like this:

Dr. John Doe   Office 237-B

SUN	MON	TUES	WED	THURS	FRI	SAT
8:00	8:00 Eng 101	8:00	8:00 Eng 101	8:00	8:00 Eng 101	8:00
9:00	9:00 Eng 102	9:00 Office	9:00 Eng 102	9:00 Office	9:00 Eng 102	9:00
10:00	10:00 Office	10:00	10:00 Office	10:00	10:00 Office	10:00
11:00	11:00 Eng 201	11:00 Office	11:00 Eng 201	11:00 Office	11:00 Eng 201	11:00
12:00	12:00 Lunch	12:00 Lunch	12:00 Lunch	12:00 Lunch	12:00 Lunch	12:00
1:00	1:00	1:00 Eng 202	1:00	1:00 Eng 202	1:00	1:00
2:00	2:00 Office	2:00	2:00 Office	2:00	2:00 Office	2:00

Looking at this schedule, when would you want to try to make an appointment with Dr. Doe? _____

For this next exercise, you may copy it from your book and use it for each professor you have. Check the schedule for each of your professors, and make an appointment with each of your professors.

During the course of your conversation, fill out this information sheet. You will get to know the professor a little better and will be able to find the professor's office when you really need to talk to him.

Professor's name _____

Professor's office location _____

Professor's office phone _____

Where did the professor go to school?

Undergraduate:_____

   Graduate: _____

   Graduate: _____

   Postgraduate: _____

How long has the professor taught at this school?_____

If the professor is ranked, what is her rank?_____

Does the professor have any special research interests? If so, what are they?

_____

_____

_____

What are the professor's hobbies? _____

_____

_____

_____

What advice could the professor give you in order to be a more successful student?_____

_____

_____

_____

    Hopefully, this exercise will allow you to see your professors as "real" people and will foster relationships with these persons outside of class. You certainly do not have to be best friends with your professors, but if you understand a little more about their backgrounds, it might make it a little easier to understand their views while you are in class.

CAMPUS RESOURCES

Observations

The life of a college professor is quite different from that of a high school teacher. Their attitude toward teaching may be different, and the emphasis they place on classroom instruction may vary from professor to professor. Rest assured, however, that most college professors are dedicated to their craft and to the world of teaching. Most professors want you to succeed and will do everything in their power to make this happen. When you put your best foot forward, your professor will certainly meet you halfway—many will go much further.

As a Result of this Chapter, and in Preparing for My Journey, I Plan to . . .

CHAPTER 11

Reaching Your Destination
Career Planning

CHAPTER 11

It is easy to live for others. Everybody does. I call on you to live for yourselves.
Ralph Waldo Emerson, poet

Grace was 56 when she first entered college. Her life had been anything but "normal." She had two grown children, had gone through a divorce, lost a home to a fire, and had just moved 1,500 miles a week before classes began. Needless to say, Grace was dealing with a great deal of stress in her life, but she was determined to become a nurse.

This had been her life-long dream.

She had not gone to college after high school but had gotten married and settled down to raise her family. When her children were older, she studied for the real estate exam and became an agent in Texas, where they were living at the time. For several years, Grace did very well. One year she made over $100,000 selling real estate. However, as the market changed and real estate became a tougher career in Texas, she lost her job and eventually moved "back home" near her family.

Grace could have continued in real estate, but her heart was not in it. She had always wanted to have a career in nursing. She enrolled in the nursing program at a local technical college and was devastated to find two major roadblocks to her dream. First, her SAT scores and her admissions test indicated that she was not academically prepared to enter the nursing curriculum, and second, there was a *three-year* waiting list to get into the *two-year* program of nursing.

After much thought and consideration, Grace decided to enroll in the transitional studies curriculum at the college and begin traveling the road to her dream. She put her name on the waiting list for the nursing program and began to take courses that would upgrade her basic skills in math, reading, and vocabulary. Over the course of the next two years, Grace hired tutors, went to study sessions, and stayed up into the late hours of the night, and finally, she passed all of the tests to admit her into the associate degree nursing program.

The phone rang one day, and the nursing department told Grace that there was an opening in the department. She was admitted almost one year earlier than she had expected. Her first course was very hard and demanding. The subject matter dealt with calculating drug doses for patients. In order to continue in the program, students *had* to pass the first test on mathematical calculations. If you failed the first test, you were removed not only from the class, but also from the nursing program. Grace failed the first test! She was asked to leave the nursing program.

Not to be beaten, Grace enrolled in a developmental math course and studied harder, stayed up longer, hired more tutors, and finally passed the course. She then enrolled in another math course and continued to build her math skills for the nursing curriculum. One year later, Grace was invited to rejoin the nursing curriculum. She enrolled in the same drug dosage calculation class. She *passed* the first test. She *passed* the second test—she *passed* the course.

Two years after re-admission, Grace walked down the isle of the local civic center to be "pinned" as a nurse. Five years after she began her journey to fulfilling her dream, she was living her dream. There were countless times when her life and experiences would have led most of us to quit, but

Grace was determined to have a career in nursing. She knew in her heart what she wanted to be "when she grew up."

What Do You Want to Be When You Grow Up?

Have you been asked that question before? Do you know the answer? You probably have given some thought to the question; maybe you have even imagined yourself doing different things. The process of career selection can be a lengthy one but is by far one of the most important things you can do for yourself. They key words here are *for yourself*. *You* are in charge here—no one else can make this decision for you. Also, this is a personal journey, one in which it is okay to "ask for directions" but also one that you control. You control the speed, and ultimately the direction your career takes you. You can change your route at any time. As a matter of fact, the world of technology and information is changing so rapidly that almost every person will change careers at least once in their lives. This was not true of your parents. In her book, *The 100 Best Jobs for the 90's and Beyond* (1994), Carol Kleiman suggests that by the year 2000, three out of ever *four* workers will need re-training for the new jobs of the next century! The decisions that you make about your career choices and the roads that you take to get there are *yours* and belong to no one else.

In the following self-study, take a few moments and determine where you stand in relation to making career decisions.

SELF-STUDY

5=Strongly Agree
4=Agree
3=Don't Know
2=Disagree
1=Strongly Disagree

1. I know what I want to be when I complete college.
   1 2 3 4 5

2. I know how to find a mentor. *1 2 3 4 5*

3. I think about my career daily. *1 2 3 4 5*

4. I would consider seeking advice from an advisor or counselor. *1 2 3 4 5*

5. I know how to use the *Dictionary of Occupational Titles*.
   1 2 3 4 5

6. I daydream about my career.
   1 2 3 4 5

7. I know how to research a career. *1 2 3 4 5*

8. I understand how shadowing works. *1 2 3 4 5*

9. I understand how personality inventories work.
   1 2 3 4 5

10. I can use a computer to help research a career.
    1 2 3 4 5

TOTAL YOUR POINTS from these ten questions. Refer to the following rating scale to determine where you stand in relation to dealing with career decision making.

0–10 You have given little to no thought about your career and your college major.

11–20 You have given some thought to your career, but you have probably done little research or planning.

21–30 Your career decision-making skills are average, but you have not put a great deal of effort into your career plans.

31–40 You have thought a lot about your career and have made an effort to find out more about your career.

41–50 You have researched your career, decided on a major, and probably shadowed someone before. Your career decision-making skills are above average.

Does your score and the rating scale match what you feel about your career decision-making skills? If not, don't worry. If you read this chapter carefully and complete the exercises within, your career decision-making skills will be enhanced.

Daydreaming

Do you like to daydream? Daydreaming can be fun and exciting. Remember how relaxing it can be to let your mind wander and travel to different places or to pretend that you are having dinner with your favorite movie star or singer? As children, we often told our friends that we were going to be doctors, lawyers, football players, or nurses. In the movie *A River Runs Through It*, two brothers are lying on the side of the river, thinking about their lives. One asks the other,

> "What are you going to be when you grow up?"
> He answers, "A professional boxer."
> "How about you?" the other brother asks.
> After some thought, he responds, "A fly fisherman."

Very few people actually do the work of their childhood dreams, like boxing and fishing and dancing and acting and being a fireman. Dreams may come true for those people who do not change their minds, but for most of us, we eventually change our minds from what we wanted as children. This is natural. However, there are those who only want to do one thing from childhood—and they *do it*.

Take a moment, clear your mind. Allow yourself to think about your first grade classroom. Remember your teacher? Do you remember talking to your friends about what you would be when you grew up? List the different occupations you may have mentioned as a child. Enjoy the journey.

1. _____
2. _____
3. _____
4. _____
5. _____

Now, think about what you have just written. Why did you, even as a child, select the occupations you listed? Take a minute and write down why you wanted to be these things.

For 1: _____
_____

Life is about change, and about movement, and about becoming something other than you are at this very moment.

Author unknown

CAREER PLANNING

For 2: _____

_____

For 3: _____

_____

For 4: _____

_____

For 5: _____

_____

Now, think for just a moment about the occupations you listed. What are your daydreams like now? What occupations do you see yourself doing now? If money were not the problem, if time in school or location or family did not play a part in your decision, and if you could do one thing for the rest of your life, what would you do? Think about that question. If money was not a part of the picture and you could do anything for the rest of your life, what would it be? List a few of those occupations in the following space. You may only have one; that's OK.

1. _____
2. _____
3. _____
4. _____
5. _____

Now, we need to take an strong look at your answer(s) and determine if you want to do something or to *be* something.

Do You Want to Do Something or Be Something?

If you were to ask most people on the street the simple question, "What do you do for a living?" They would respond, "I'm a welder" or "I'm an engineer" or "I'm a teacher." Most people answer the question without ever thinking about what is really being asked.

> *I went into the woods because I wished to live deliberately, to front only the essential facts of life, and see if I could not learn what it had to teach, and not, when I came to die, discover that I had not lived.*
>
> **Henry David Thoreau, author and naturalist**

This is one of the first questions that you will need to examine when deciding on a career. Do I want to *do* something, or do I want to *be* something. Just because a person has a certain title, such as welder or engineer or teacher, the title alone does not make them *be* a welder or engineer or teacher. The art of *being* is a mind-set that is developed on your own. There are many people who teach for a living, but there are very few "teachers." There are people who do social work, but few are actually "social workers." To *be* something, you have to make a philosophical decision regarding your future. The questions you have to ask are, "How do I want to spend my time?" and "What is my purpose in life?" As an individual, you can *do* almost anything. You can do the work of medicine, you can do the work of upholding the law, you can do the work of instruction, but in order to *be* a doctor, lawyer, or teacher, you have to want to *become* the epitome for which those professions stand. Doing the work is not enough to bring fulfillment to your life; doing is the easy part. Being the person who heals, protects justice, or teaches will bring you joy.

There is an old story about a stranger who was walking down the road one day when he came upon three men cutting

CAREER PLANNING 249

stone. He stopped to asked the first man what he was doing. "I'm cutting these rocks in half, can't you see that?" The stranger approached the second man cutting stone and asked that gentleman what he was doing. "I'm shaping these stones into blocks, can't you see?" Finally, the stranger came upon the third stone cutter and stopped to ask him what he was doing. Replied the last stone cutter, "I'm building a cathedral, can't you see?"

Where it takes only physical strength to do something, it takes vision to be something. So, what do you want to be? Have you decided? If not, there's help for the undeclared.

Not all who wander are lost.

J.R.R. Tolkien, author

Help Me! I'm Undeclared!

No, it isn't a fatal disease. You're not dying. Being undeclared is not a disgrace, nor is it a weakness. It is a temporary state of mind, and the best way to deal with it is to stop and think. A person should never declare a major simply because she is ashamed to be undeclared. Also, you should never allow yourself to be pressured into declaring a major. There are certain measures that you can take to work toward declaring a major and being satisfied with your decision.

Seven Steps to Career Decision Making

STEP ONE: DREAM!

As questioned earlier, if money was not a problem or concern, what would you do for the rest of your life? If you could do anything in the world, what would you do, where would you do it? These are the types of questions that you should ask yourself as you try to select a major and career. Let your mind wander, and let the sky be the limit. Write your dreams down. These dreams may be closer to reality than you know. In the words of Don Quixote, "Let us dream, my soul, let us dream" (Unamuno).

STEP TWO: TALK TO YOUR ADVISOR

Academic advisors are there to help you. Do not, however, be surprised if some of their doors are closed. First, always make an appointment to see an advisor. They teach, conduct research, perform community service, and sometimes advise in excess of a hundred students. Always call in advance. However, when you have an appointment, make that advisor work for you. Take your college catalog and ask questions, hard questions. Your advisor will not make a career decision for you, but if you ask the proper questions, the advisor can be of monumental importance to you and your career decisions.

You will also want to use students in your program as advisors. They will prove to be invaluable to you as you work your way through the daily workings of the college. Upperclassmen can assist you in making decisions regarding your classes, electives, and college work study programs. They can even help you join and become an active member of a preprofessional program.

STEP THREE: USING COLLEGE ELECTIVES

Most accreditation agencies working with your college require that you be allowed at least one free elective in your degree program. Some programs allow many more. Use your electives wisely! Taking courses just to get the hours can be a waste of time. The wisest students will use their electives to delve into new areas of interest, or take a block of courses in another area that might enhance their career decisions. Perhaps you are interested in business; you may want to use your first elective to take an introduction to business course. Maybe you need to use your first elective(s) to take an art course or a music course or even one in psychology. Be creative, be courageous, be wild, but don't play it safe. Take a chance. It can be the best thing that ever happened to you. One of these electives might be the key to choosing your career.

STEP FOUR: GO TO THE CAREER CENTER

Even the smallest colleges have some type of career center or a career counselor. *Use them!* Most of the time, career centers on campus are free. If you go into the community for the same type of services, you could pay anywhere from $200 to $2,000. The professionals in the career center can show you information on a variety of careers and work fields. They can administer certain interest and personality inventories that can help you make career and major decisions.

STEP FIVE: READ! READ! READ!

Nothing will help you more than reading about careers and majors. Ask your advisor or counselor to help you locate as much information on your areas of interest as possible. Gather information from colleges, agencies, associations, and places of employment. Then *read it!*

STEP SIX: SHADOWING

No, this is not what vampires do when the full moon is out. This is a term used to describe the process of following someone around on the job. Perhaps you have an interest in the field of medicine, but you don't know exactly what a general practitioner does all day. It might be possible for you to ask your doctor if you could spend the day with her and "shadow" her activities. You might call an engineering office and ask if you can sit with several of their engineers for a day over spring break. This is the *very best* way to get first-hand, honest information regarding a profession in which you might be interested. You might ask questions like: Why do you do this for a living? What training do you have? How long did you go to school in order to get this job? What is your salary range? Is there room for growth? What is your greatest achievement on this job? What was your weakest moment?

STEP SEVEN: JOINING PREPROFESSIONAL ORGANIZATIONS

One of the most important decisions you will make as a college student is getting involved in organizations and clubs on campus that offer educational opportunities, social interaction, and hands-on experience in your chosen field. Preprofessional organizations can open doors that will assist you in making a career decision, growing in your field, meeting professionals already working in your field, and eventually getting a job.

Another important aspect of studying and researching a career is finding a mentor with whom you can work and can shadow.

What Is a Mentor?

ebster's Collegiate Dictionary defines mentor as "a trusted counselor or guide; a tutor or guide."

Jimmie's Story

I remember my first mentor—a gentleman that served as provost at the college I attended. Dr. Thomas was everything I wanted to be—successful, self-assured, intelligent, and fun loving. He had achieved so much during his career, was well-traveled, but still had not lost the "common touch." He could relate to anyone on any level and was an excellent judge of character. I soon realized that not only was he my professional mentor, but also my mental and emotional mentor. I depended on his advice and his friendship and find myself wishing that he was still alive today to offer advice about my career and about my life in general.

These thoughts truly define what a mentor can mean to a student. Mentors have been around for ages. Scholars had young students study under their guidance, and soon the young students became scholars themselves. Mentors can be anyone that you admire professionally, personally, mentally, or socially.

CAREER PLANNING

When trying to imagine what a mentor is, it might be helpful to explore what a mentor is *not*. In this case, a mentor is not an idol or god to be revered. This person should be someone with whom you feel comfortable and in whom you can trust. When you become successful, you will be a professional peer to this individual if your career follows the same course. A mentor does not necessarily have to be a great deal older than you. People can be mentors at any age, and you are never too old to have a mentor. It is important that you eventually let the person know that you see them as your mentor. If for no other reason, you let them know that you value who they are and what they have achieved.

Think for just a moment about mentors in your life. As you do, list any mentors you may have and tell why you respect this person:

1. _____

Why do you admire this person? _____
_____

2. _____

Why do you admire this person? _____
_____

3. _____

Why do you admire this person? _____
_____

Make the decision right now that you will let the people listed know that you admire them. You will be surprised at the reaction it could bring. You may very well be making the first professional contacts of your career—contacts that can help you find jobs as your career progresses.

Now, reflect back on all of the responses you have listed. Are you being influenced by another person or by an idea about a career? How much *original* thought have you given to career selection? Many people end up majoring in a certain discipline because a friend is majoring in that field or because a parent or grandparent majored in that field. Remember, one of the most important decisions you will *ever* make in your life is choosing a career. The decision should be your own. If you are still having some trouble thinking about a career or narrowing your focus, you might consider seeking the advice and assistance of a career counselor.

What Is a Career Counselor?

A career counselor could be viewed as a career travel agent of sorts. This person can help you understand the variety of options that you might have and can help you map your way. Career counselors can help you learn more about yourself and help you clarify goals for the future. Career counselors can be located in schools, colleges, and in the private sector. They will assist you with the processes outlined earlier, but you must remember that ultimately, *you* are in charge. You may want to ask your counselor to administer the Myers-Briggs Personality Type Indicator or the Strong-Campbell Interest Inventory to assist you with this process. These instruments give you an idea of who you are and for what type of work you are best suited. If your counselor or college cannot provide this kind of assistance to you, look for private companies in your area that can.

An interesting and educational way to learn more about your career of choice is to write an "I Search paper." An I Search paper is a research project in which you search for information relating to your career. You should ask the basic questions about who, what, where, and when. Find someone who is actively involved in the career you want to find out more about and search them out. Find out all you can about their career, and then write a paper about your experience. Share copies of your paper with other members of your class. You might find someone in the class who even has the same interest as you. This is one more way to develop a mentor. At the end of this chapter, you will find a model from which you can build your I Search paper.

Once You Know Where You Are Going, How Do You Get There?

The next step in this process is *research*. This is where *you* come in. Deciding to do the research will yield remarkable results.

This process is lengthy and if done correctly, can take *lots* of time, especially if you want to examine several careers.

First, spend some time listing the careers from the Career Interests Inventories or Personality Inventories you have completed at your school's career center. If you have not completed an inventory, look back at your mentor list and your dream list. Develop a list of careers that you wish to explore.

After you have identified a career in which you are interested, the research begins. Look at the *Dictionary of Occupational Titles* (DOT). This is usually available in the reference section of your library. Look up the careers that you have selected. Read every bit of information you can on these careers—take notes. While looking at the DOT, you will want to answer the questions found in the "Roadways to Career Decision Making" section of this chapter.

Will I Work with People, Things, or Ideas?

This is a most important question. Do you enjoy working with people, or do you enjoy working with machinery. If someone is a "people person," and he is working with machines all day, he is probably not going to be very happy. The same is true for someone who does not enjoy working directly with people, but he finds himself doing so daily. Make your career fit your personality.

How Much Training Am I Going to Need to Do this Job?

For some students, the answer to this question will determine what they do for the rest of their lives. Some people are not interested in going to college, or if they do, they only want a two-year degree or a certificate. Others do not mind going to college for ten or twelve years. This decision is up to you. It is important to note, however, that according to *US News and World Report*, students who attend college at any level and graduate tend to earn more than those students who do not attend.

How Much Money Will I Make in this Profession?

Recently, I had a friend who was offered a job making $90,000 per year—for *nine* months' work. She did not take the job because she told me that money did not motivate her. She said, "My family is here, my friends are here, my church is here, and I love the weather. I'm not going to take it . . . I wouldn't be happy." For some people, money will be a driving force. For others, money will not matter at all. This decision is up to you.

Do I Know Anyone Who Already Works in this Profession?

It is always good to talk to people who already work in the profession in which you are interested. Go to that person and ask them questions about money, raises, promotions, work atmosphere, climate, and overall satisfaction. This information may help you make some hard decisions about your career.

Will I Work Indoors or Outdoors?

For many people, this question is the driving force behind their career decisions. Nothing could be worse than a person who loves the outdoors being trapped behind a desk for eight to ten hours a day. On the other hand, if someone does not enjoy outdoors, she would be miserable working construction or in the areas of wildlife or forestry.

Will the Work I Do Be Mental or Physical?

Again, this depends on you as an individual. Some people love to work with heavy objects and use their bodies. Others love to think and work with their minds daily. Usually, you are going to find jobs that require that you do a little of both. You should always use your mind, but some jobs require that you use it more often and in different ways.

Where Will I Live While Doing this Job?

Some people do not care if they have to move far away to do their work. Others prefer to stay in the area in which they were born. Some people love the colder climate of the north, while others would rather live near the beach. The answer to this question could determine your career as well. You would have a hard time being an ocean diver or deep sea fisherman if you lived in Utah.

Will I Travel with this Job?

Some people feel that one of the most exciting things in the world is constant travel. They almost move from one hotel to the next and love every minute of every new city. Others do not enjoy this lifestyle at all. They would prefer to have a job that does not require them to travel at all. Again, you must evaluate your own preference.

Would I Want to Do this for the Rest of My Life?

Think about your career choices. Do you see yourself doing this job for the rest of your life? That is a long time, hopefully. Would you be happy to look back on your life and say, "This is what I did for a living; this is how I made my mark on the world"?

These are some important issues and questions that you must answer when researching and considering a career. There is a place at the end of this chapter to answer these questions about your life's work.

Develop a Personal Success Plan

Now that you have all of your directions, write them down and place them where you will be able to refer to them often. Some career consultants suggests the following format for a personal success plan:

Success Plan Outline

Write goals.

CAREER PLANNING

Make an appointment to see an advisor (counselor).

Visit your school career center.

Research your interests at the library.

Read about your interests.

Take classes that interest you as electives.

Find someone to shadow.

Tell others about your dreams.

Review your goals.

Finally, you should realize that there are numerous places to find information regarding careers, majors, professions, and the world of work. Listed next are just a few of the places you should look when examining careers:

College counseling centers

The *Dictionary of Occupational Titles*

The *Guide for Occupational Exploration*

What Color is your Parachute? (book by Bolles)

The Three Boxes of Life (book by Bolles)

The United States Armed Forces

The Holland Self-Directed Search

The Myers-Briggs Personality Type Indicator

Computer data bases such as SIGI, SIGI Plus, or DISCOVER

Observations

You are in charge here. Whatever you become, whatever you make of yourself, is ultimately a choice that *you* make. Your decisions will be with you for the rest of your life. A career is more than a job. A career is a state of mind that leads to your life's work. As you begin your personal journey, remember this quote by the famous writer, George Bernard Shaw:

People are always blaming their circumstances for what they are. I don't believe in circumstances. The people who get on in this world are the people who get up and look for the circumstances they want, and, if they can't find them, then make them.

My Career Research Plan

Career to be researched: _____

Why am I interested in this career? _____
_____
_____
_____

Will I work with people or things? _____
_____
_____
_____

How much training is required? _____
_____
_____
_____

How much money will I make? _____
_____
_____
_____

Who do I know already working in this field? _____
_____

What did they say about this profession? _____
_____
_____

Will I work indoors or outdoors? _____
_____
_____

Will the work be mental or physical? _____
_____
_____

Where will I live to do this work? _____
_____
_____

Will this work involve much travel? _____
_____
_____

The best thing I found out about this profession is _____
_____
_____
_____

The worst thing I found out about this profession is _____
_____
_____
_____
_____

Sources of my research: _____
_____
_____

People I interviewed: _____
_____
_____
_____

As a Result of this Chapter, and in Preparing for My Journey, I Plan to . . .

CAREER PLANNING

REFERENCES

Adler, R., Rosenfeld, L., & Towne, N. (1989). *Interplay, The Process of Interpersonal Communication*, 4th ed. New York: Holt, Rinehart and Winston.

Barranger, M. (1994). *Understanding Plays*, 2nd ed. Boston: Allyn and Bacon.

Bits and Pieces, Vol. N, No. 2. Fairfield, NJ: The Economic Press.

Ellis, D., Lankowitz, S., Stupka, E., & Toft, D. *Career Planning.* (1990). Rapid City, IA: College Survival.

Gardner, J., & Jewler, J. (1989). *Your College Experience*. Belmont, CA: Wadsworth.

Kleiman, C. *The 100 Best Jobs for the 90's and Beyond*. (1992). New York: Berkley Books.

GLOSSARY
The Language for Success in College

A

ACADEMIC FREEDOM Academic freedom allows professors in institutions of higher education to conduct research and teach their findings, even if the subject matter is controversial. Academic freedom gives college professors the right to teach certain materials that might not be allowed in high school.

ACCREDITATION Most high schools and colleges in the United States receive accreditation from a regional agency, which ensures that all its members meet or exceed a minimum set of standards. The Southern Association of Colleges and Schools is an accreditation agency.

ADDING Adding a class means enrolling in an additional class. The term is usually used during registration period or during the first week of a semester.

ADMINISTRATION The administration of a college is headed by the president and vice presidents and comprises the nonteaching personnel who handle all administrative aspects of running the college. The structure of the administration varies at each college.

ADVISING An academic advisor is assigned to each student on arrival on campus. It is the advisor's responsibility to guide students through their academic work at the college, to be sure that they know what classes to take and in what order. An advisor is most often a faculty member in the student's discipline or major who will work with the student through the student's entire college career.

AFRICAN-AMERICAN STUDIES Courses in African-American studies consider the major contributions of African-Americans in art, literature, history, medicine, sciences, and architecture. Many colleges offer majors and minors in African-American studies.

AIDS This acronym stands for acquired immunodeficiency syndrome, a disease that is transmitted sexually, intravenously, or from mother to fetus. There is currently no known cure for AIDS, but several medications, such as AZT, ddC, 3TC, dT4, Saquinavir, ddI, and Indinavir, help to slow the deterioration of the immune system. AIDS is the number-one killer of people aged 25 to 44 years.

ALUMNA, ALUMNUS, ALUMNI These terms describe people who attended a college. *Alumna* refers to a woman, *alumnus* refers to men, and *alumni* refers to more than one of either or both. The term *alumni* is the most often used.

AMERICA ONLINE America Online (AOL) is the nation's largest commercial on-line computer service. It offers a gateway to the Internet, magazines, software, live interactive services, and financial services, and can be one of the most informative and exciting learning tools for college students.

ARTICULATION An articulation agreement is a document signed by representatives of two or more institutions that guarantees that courses taken at one of the participating institutions will be accepted by the others. For example, if Oak College has an articulation agreement with Maple College, course work completed at Oak College will be accepted toward a degree at Maple College.

ASSOCIATE DEGREE An associate degree is a two-year degree that usually prepares the student to enter the workforce with a specific skill or trade. It is also offered to students as the first two years of a bachelor's, or four-year, degree program. Not all colleges offer the associate degree.

ATTENDANCE Every college has an attendance policy, such as, "Any student who misses more than 10% of the total class hours will receive an F for the course." This policy is followed strictly by some professors and more leniently by others. Students should know the attendance policy of each professor with whom they are studying.

AUDITING Most colleges offer the option of auditing a course. Whereas a student enrolled in a course pays a fee, must attend classes, takes exams, and receives credit, a student auditing a course usually pays a smaller fee, does not have to take exams, and does not receive credit. People who are having trouble in a subject or who simply want to gain more knowledge about a subject but don't need or want credit are the most likely candidates for auditing. Some colleges charge full price for auditing a course.

B

BACCALAUREATE The baccalaureate degree, more commonly called the bachelor's degree, is a four-year degree granted in a specific field, although it can be completed in as few as three or as many as six or more years. This degree prepares students for careers in such fields as education, social work, engineering, fine arts, and journalism.

BOARD OF TRUSTEES The board of trustees is the governing body of a college. For state schools, the board is appointed by government officials (usually the governor) of the state. The board hires the president, must approve any curriculum changes to degree programs, and sets policy for the college.

C

CAMPUS The term *campus* refers to the physical plant of a university or college, including all buildings, fields, arenas, auditoriums, and other properties owned by the college.

CAMPUS POLICE All colleges and universities have a campus police or security office. Campus security helps students with problems ranging from physical danger to car trouble. Every student should know where this office is in case of emergency.

CARREL A carrel is a booth or small room, often large enough to accommodate one person only, located in the library. Students and faculty can reserve a carrel for professional use by the semester or the week. Personal belongings and important academic materials should never be left in a carrel, because they could be stolen.

CATALOG The college catalog is a legal, binding document that states the degree requirements of the college. It is issued to all students at the beginning of their college career, and it is essential to developing a schedule and completing a degree program. Students must keep the catalog of the year in which they entered college.

CERTIFICATE A certificate program is a series of courses, usually lasting one year, designed to educate and train an individual in a specific area, such as welding, automotive repair, medical transcription, tool and die, early childhood, physical therapy, and fashion merchandising. Although certified and detailed, these programs are not degree programs. Associate and bachelor's degrees are also offered in many of the areas that have certificate programs.

CLEP The College Level Examination Program (CLEP) allows students to test out of a course. The exams are nationally averaged and are often more extensive than a course in the same area. If a student CLEPs a course, it means the student does not have to take the course in which he or she passed the CLEP exam.

COGNATE A cognate is a course or set of courses taken outside of the student's major but usually in a field related to the major. Some colleges call this a minor. A student majoring in English, may take a cognate in history or drama.

COMMUNICATIONS College curricula often mandate nine hours of communications, which commonly refers to English and speech (oral communication) courses. The mixture of courses is typically English 101 and 102 and Speech 101; the numbers vary from college to college.

COMPREHENSIVE EXAMS Exams that encompass materials from the entire course are comprehensive exams. That is, a comprehensive exam covers information from the first lecture through the last.

CONTINUING EDUCATION Continuing education or community education courses are designed to meet specific business and industry needs or to teach subjects of interest to the community. These courses are not offered for college credit, but continuing education units may be awarded. Continuing education courses range from small engine repair to flower arranging, from stained glass making to small business management.

CO-OP This term refers to a relationship between a business or industry and the educational institution that allows a student to spend a semester in college and the next semester on the job. Co-ops may be structured in various ways, but the general idea of a co-op is always to gain on-the-job experience while in college.

CO-REQUISITE A co-requisite is a course that must be taken at the same time as another course. Science courses often carry a co-requisite, for example, Biology 101 may have as a co-requisite the lab course, Biology 101L.

COUNSELING Most college campuses have a counseling center staffed by counselors trained to assist students with problems that might arise in their personal lives, with their study skills, and with their career aspirations. Counseling is different from advising; academic advisors are responsible for helping students with their academic progress. Some colleges combine the two, but in most cases the counselor and the advisor are two different people with two different job descriptions.

COURSE TITLE Every course has a course title. A schedule of classes may read: ENG 101, SPC 205,

HIS 210, and so on. The college catalog defines what these terms mean. For example, ENG 101 usually stands for English 101, SPC could be the heading for speech, HIS could mean history. Headings and course titles vary from college to college.

CREDIT HOUR A credit hour is the amount of credit earned for a class. Most classes are worth three credit hours; science, foreign language, and some math courses that require labs are worth four credit hours. A class that carries three credit hours typically meets for three hours per week. This formula varies in summer sessions or midsessions.

CURRICULUM The curriculum is a set of classes that the student must take to earn a degree in an area of study.

D

DEAN *Dean* is the title given to the head of a division or area of study. The dean is the policy maker and usually the business manager and final decision maker for that area. A college might have a dean of arts and sciences, a dean of business, and a dean of mathematics. Deans usually report to a vice-president or provost.

DEAN'S LIST The dean's list is a listing of students who have achieved at least a 3.5 (B+) on a 4.0 scale (see definition of numbers in entry "GPA"). Although it varies from college to college, the dean's list generally comprises students in the top 5% of the college.

DEGREE A student is awarded a degree for completing an approved course of study. The type of degree depends on the college, the number of credit hours in the program, and the field of study. A two-year degree is called an associate degree, and a four-year degree is called a bachelor's degree. A student who attends graduate school may receive a master's degree (after two to three years) and a doctorate (after three to ten years). Some colleges offer postdoctorate degrees.

DIPLOMA A diploma is awarded when an approved course of study is completed. Diploma requirements are not as detailed or comprehensive as the requirements for an associate degree and usually consist of only eight to twelve courses specific to a certain field.

DROPPING Students may elect to drop a class if they are not enjoying it or think that they will not be able to pass it because of grades or absenteeism. A class that has been dropped will no longer appear on the student's schedule or be calculated in the GPA. Rules and regulations governing dropping courses vary from college to college and are explained in the college catalog.

E

ELECTIVE An elective is a course that a student chooses to take outside his or her major field of study. An elective can be in an area of interest to the student or in an area that complements the student's major. For example, an English major might choose an elective in the field of theater or history because these fields complement one another. An English major might also elect to take a course in medical terminology because of an interest in that area.

EMERITI This Latin term applies to retired college personnel who have performed exemplary duties during their professional careers. A college president who procured funding for new buildings, enhanced curriculum programs, and increased the endowment might be named president emeritus (singular of emeriti) on retirement.

EVENING COLLEGE An evening college program is designed to allow students who have full-time jobs to enroll in classes that meet in the evening. Some colleges offer an entire degree program in the evening; others offer only some courses in the evening.

F

FACULTY The faculty is the body of professionals at a college who teach, conduct research, and perform community service. Faculty members prepare for many years to hold the responsibilities carried by the title. Some may have studied for 25 years or more to obtain the knowledge and skill necessary to train students in their specific fields.

FEES *Fees* refers to the money charged by colleges for specific items and services. Fees may be charged for tuition, meal plans, books, health care, and activities. Fees vary from college to college and are usually printed in the college catalog.

FINANCIAL AID Financial aid is money awarded to a student from the college, state or federal government, private sources, or places of employment on the basis of need or of merit. Any grant, loan, or scholarship is formally called financial aid.

FINE ARTS The fine arts encompass a variety of artistic forms, such as theater, dance, architecture, drawing, painting, sculpture, and music. Some colleges also include literature in this category.

FIRST-YEAR STUDENT The term *first-year student* is used by colleges and refers to a student who has not yet completed 30 semester hours of college-level work.

FOREIGN LANGUAGE Almost every college offers at least one course in foreign language, and many colleges offer degrees in this area. Some of the many foreign languages offered in U.S. colleges are Spanish, French, Russian, Latin, German, Portuguese, Swahili, Arabic, Japanese, Chinese, and Korean.

FRATERNITY A fraternity is an organization in the Greek system. Fraternities are open to male students only. Induction for each is different. Many fraternities have their own housing complexes on campus. Honorary fraternities, such as Phi Kappa Phi, are academic in nature and are open to men and women.

G

GPA The grade point average, GPA, is the numerical grading system used by most colleges in the United States. A student's GPA determines his or her eligibility for continued enrollment, financial aid, and honors. Most colleges operate under a 4.0 system: an A is worth 4 quality points, a B 3 points, a C 2 points, a D 1 point, and an F 0 points. To calculate a GPA, for each course, the number of quality points earned is multiplied by the number of credit hours carried by the course; the numbers thus obtained for all courses are added together; finally, this total is divided by the total number of hours carried.

Example: A student is taking English 101, Speech 101, History 201, and Psychology 101, all of which carry three credit hours. If the student earns all A's, the GPA is 4.0; if the student earns all B's, the GPA is 3.0. However, if he or she had a variety of grades, you would calculate the GPA as such:

COURSE	GRADE	CREDIT HRS		QUALITY POINTS	TOTAL POINTS
ENG 101	A	3	x	4	= 12 points
SPC 101	C	3	x	2	= 6 points
HIS 201	B	3	x	3	= 9 points
PSY 101	D	3	x	1	= 3 points

GPA = 30 points divided by 12 hours = 2.5 (C+)

GRADUATE TEACHING ASSISTANT In some larger colleges and universities, students working toward master's and doctorate degrees teach lower level undergraduate classes under the direction of a senior professor in the department.

GRANT Usually a grant is money and goes toward tuition and books and does not have to be repaid. Grants are most often awarded by state and federal governments.

H

HIGHER EDUCATION This term applies to any level of education beyond high school; all colleges are considered institutions of higher education.

HONOR CODE Many colleges operate under an honor code, which demands that students perform all work without cheating, plagiarizing, or engaging in any other dishonest actions. A student who breaks the honor code may be expelled from the institution. In some cases, a student may be expelled if he or she does not turn in a fellow student whom he or she knows has broken the code.

HONORS Academic honors are based on a student's GPA. Academic honors may include the dean's list, the president's list, and departmental honors. The three highest honors, summa cum laude, magna cum laude, and cum laude, are awarded at graduation to students who have maintained a GPA of 3.5 or better. Although the breakdown varies from college to college, these honors are usually awarded as follows: cum laude, 3.5 to 3.7; magna cum laude, 3.7 to 3.9; and summa cum laude, 4.0.

HONORS COLLEGE The honors college is a degree or a set of classes offered for students who performed exceptionally in high school.

HUMANITIES The humanities are sometimes as misunderstood as the fine arts. Disciplines in the humanities include history, philosophy, religion, cultural studies, and sometimes literature, government, and foreign languages. The college catalog defines what a college designates as humanities.

I

IDENTIFICATION CARDS An identification (ID) card is an essential possession for any college student. An ID card allows students to use the library, participate in activities, use physical fitness facilities, and often, attend events free of charge. ID cards can also be useful beyond the campus borders. Admission to movie theaters, museums, zoos, and cultural events usually costs less and is sometimes free for students with IDs. ID cards also allow access to most area library facilities with special privileges. Some colleges issue ID cards at no charge, and some charge a small fee. ID cards are usually validated each semester.

INDEPENDENT STUDY Many colleges offer some independent study options. Independent study courses have no formal classes and no classroom teacher; students work independently to complete the course under the general guidelines of the department and with the assistance of an instructor. Colleges often require that students maintain a minimum GPA in order to enroll in independent study classes.

J

JOURNAL In many classes, such as English, orientation, literature, history, and psychology, students are required to keep a journal of thoughts, opinions, research, and class discussions. The journal often serves as a communication link between the student and the professor.

JUNIOR A student who is in his or her third year of college or who has completed at least 60 credit hours of study is a junior.

L

LECTURE The lecture is the lesson given by an instructor in a class. Some instructors use group discussions, peer tutoring, or multimedia presentations. The term *lecture* is usually used when the material is presented in a lecture format, that is, when the professor presents most of the information.

LIBERAL ARTS A liberal arts curriculum ensures that the students are exposed to a variety of disciplines and cultural experiences, that they take courses beyond those needed for a specific vocation or occupation. A student at a liberal arts college who is majoring in biology would also have to take courses in fine arts, history, social sciences, math, hard sciences, and other areas.

LOAD The number of credit hours or classes that a student is taking is the student's load. The normal load is between 15 and 18 hours, or five to six classes. In most colleges, 12 hours is considered a full-time load, but a student can take up to 18 or 21 hours for the same tuition.

M

MAJOR A major is a student's intended field of study. The term *major* indicates that the majority of the student's work will be completed in that field. Students are usually required to declare a major by the end of their sophomore (second) year.

MEAL PLAN A student purchases a meal plan at the beginning of a semester that allows him or her to eat certain meals in the cafeteria or dining hall. These plans are regulated by a computer card or punch system. Meal plans can be purchased for three meals a day, breakfast only, lunch only, or a variety of other meal combinations.

MENTOR A mentor is someone who can help a student through troubled times, assist in decision making, and provide advice. A mentor can be a teacher, staff member, fellow classmate, or upper level student. Mentors seldom volunteer. They usually fall into the role of mentor because they are easy to talk with, knowledgeable about the college and the community, and willing to lend a helping hand. Sometimes students are assigned mentors when they arrive on campus.

MINOR A student's minor usually comprises six to eight courses in a specific field that complements the student's major area of study. A student majoring in engineering might minor in math or electronics, subjects that might help later in the workforce.

N

NATURAL SCIENCES The *natural and physical sciences* refer to a select group of courses from biology, chemistry, physical science, physics, anatomy, zoology, botany, geology, genetics, microbiology, physiology, and astronomy.

O

ORIENTATION All students are invited and many are required to attend an orientation session when they enter college. These sessions are extremely useful. They present important information about college life as well as details of the rules of the specific college.

P

PLAGIARISM *Plagiarism* refers to the act of using another person's words or works as one's own without citing the original author. Penalties for plagiarism vary and can include asking the student to withdraw from the institution. Most institutions have strict guidelines for dealing with plagiarism. Penalties for plagiarism are usually listed in the student handbook.

PREFIX The code used by the Office of the Registrar to designate a certain area of study is called a prefix. Common prefixes are ENG for English, REL for Religion, THE for Theater, and HIS for History. Prefix lettering varies from college to college.

PREPROFESSIONAL PROGRAMS Preprofessional programs usually refer to majors that require further study at the master's or doctoral level in order to be able to practice in the field. Such programs include law, medicine, dentistry, psychiatry, nursing, veterinary studies, and theology.

PREREQUISITE A prerequisite is a course that must be taken before another course. For example, in most colleges students are required to take English 101 and 102 (Composition I and II) before taking any literature courses. Therefore, English 101 and 102 are prerequisites to literature. Prerequisites are listed in the college catalog.

PRESIDENT A college president is the visionary leader of the institution. He or she is usually hired by the board of trustees. The president's primary responsibilities include financial planning, fundraising, developing community relations, and maintaining the academic integrity of the curriculum. Every employee at the college is responsible to the president.

PROBATION A student who has not performed well in his or her academic studies, usually manifested by a GPA below 2.0 in any given semester or quarter, may be placed on academic probation for one semester. If the student continues to perform below 2.0, he or she may be suspended. The rules for probation and suspension must be displayed in the college catalog.

PROFESSOR Not all teachers at the college level are professors. The system of promotion among college teachers is adjunct instructor, instructor, lecturer, assistant professor, associate professor, and full professor or professor. A full professor is likely to have been in the profession for a long time and usually holds a doctorate degree.

PROVOST The provost of a college is the primary policy maker with regard to academic standards. The provost usually reports directly to the president. Many colleges do not have provosts, but have instead a vice-president for academic affairs or a dean of instruction.

R

READMIT A student who has stopped out for a semester or two, usually has to be readmitted to the college, but does not lose previously earned academic credit unless the credit carried a time limit. Some courses in psychology, for example, carry a five- or ten-year limit, which means that the course must be retaken if a degree is not awarded within that time period. Students who elect not to attend summer sessions do not need to be readmitted. There is typically no application fee for a readmitted student.

REGISTRAR The registrar has one of the most difficult jobs on any college campus, because the registrar is responsible for all student academic records as well as for entering all grades, recording all drops and adds, printing the schedule, and verifying all candidates for graduation. The Office of the Registrar is sometimes referred to as the records office.

RESIDENCE HALL A residence hall is a facility on campus where students live. Residence halls can be single sex or coeducational. Many new students choose to live in residence halls because they are conveniently located and they provide a good way to meet new friends and become involved in extracurricular activities. Each residence hall usually has a full-time supervisor and elects a student representative to the student council. In addition, a director of student housing oversees the residence halls.

RESIDENCY REQUIREMENT Many colleges have a residency requirement; that is, they require that a minimum number of credits must be earned at the home institution. Many two-year colleges require that at least 50% of credits applied toward graduation must be earned at the home college. Many four-year colleges require that the last 30 hours of credits must be earned at the home college. All residency requirements are spelled out in the college catalog.

ROOM AND BOARD *Room and board* refers to a place to stay and food to eat. Colleges often charge students who live on campus a fee for room and board. Students may opt to buy a meal plan along with their dorm room. Issues involving room and board are usually discussed during orientation.

S

SCHOLAR *Scholar* typically refers to a student who has performed in a superior manner in a certain field of study.

SECTION CODE When many sections of the same course are offered, a section code identifies the hour and instructor of the student's particular class. A schedule that includes section codes may look something like this:

English 101 01 MWF 8:00–8:50 Smith
English 101 02 MWF 8:00–8:50 Jones
English 101 03 T TH 8:00–9:15 McGee

The numbers 01, 02, 03, and so on refer to a specific section of 101.

SENIOR *Senior* refers to a student who is in the last year of study for the undergraduate degree. To be a senior, a student must have completed at least 90 credit hours.

SOCIAL SCIENCES The social sciences study society and people. Social science courses may include psychology, sociology, anthropology, political science, geography, economics, and international studies.

SOPHOMORE *Sophomore* refers to a student who is in the second year of study and who has completed at least 30 credit hours.

SORORITIES A sorority is an organization in the Greek system that is open to women only. Many sororities have on-campus housing complexes. Initiation into a sorority differs from organization to organization and from campus to campus.

STAFF College personnel are usually divided into three categories: administration, staff, and faculty. The staff is responsible for the day-to-day workings of the college. People who work in admissions, financial aid, the bookstore, housing, student activities, and personnel, for example, usually hold staff titles, whereas the people who head these departments are usually in administration.

STUDENT GOVERNMENT ASSOCIATION One of the most powerful and visible organizations on the college campus, the Student Government Association (SGA) usually comprises students from all four undergraduate classes. Officers are elected annually. The SGA is the student voice on campus and represents the entire student body before the administration of the college.

STUDENT LOAN A student loan is money that must be repaid. Student loans generally have a much lower rate of interest than do bank loans, and the payment schedule for most student loans does not begin until six months after graduation. This delayed start is intended to allow the graduate to find a secure job and a steady income before having to make payments. If a student decides to return to school, the loan can be deferred, with additional interest, until the graduate degree is completed.

SUSPENSION Students may be suspended for a variety of reasons, but most suspensions are for academic reasons. Again, GPA requirements vary, but students are usually suspended if their GPA falls below 1.5 for two consecutive semesters. The college catalog lists the rules regarding suspension.

SYLLABUS In college, a syllabus replaces the class outline of high school. A syllabus is a legally binding contract between the student and the professor; it contains the attendance policy, the grading scale, the required text, the professor's office hours and phone number(s), and important, relevant information about the course. Most professors include the class operational calendar as a part of the syllabus. The syllabus is one of the most important documents that is issued in a class. Students should take the syllabus to class daily and keep it at least until the semester is over.

T

TENURE Tenure basically guarantees a professor lifelong employment at an institution. Tenure is usually awarded to professors who have been with the college for many years in recognition of their successful efforts in research, their record of having books and articles published, and their community service.

TOEFL The Test of English as a Foreign Language, TOEFL, is used to certify that international students have the English skills necessary to succeed at the institution or to become a teaching assistant. Some colleges allow international students to use English to satisfy their foreign language requirement if they score high enough on the TOEFL.

TRANSCRIPT A transcript is a formal record of all work attempted and/or completed at a college. A student has a transcript for every college attended. Many colleges have a policy of listing all classes, completed or not, on the transcript. Some colleges allow Ds and Fs to be removed if the student repeats the course and earns a better grade, but many others retain the original grade and continue to calculate it in the GPA. Rules regarding transcripts vary from college to college. Many employers now require that a prospective employee furnish a college transcript.

TRANSIENT A transient student is a student who is taking one or two courses at a college other than his or her home institution. For example, a student who enrolls in a college near home for the summer while maintaining student status at his or her chosen college is a transient student.

TRANSITIONAL STUDIES Many colleges have an open admission policy, meaning that the door is open to any student, and colleges frequently offer a transitional studies program to help students reach their educational goals. For example, a student who has not performed well in English, math, or reading may be required to attend a transitional studies class to upgrade basic skills in that area.

TRANSFER The term *transfer* can refer to course work as well as to students. A student who enrolls in one college and then moves to another is classified as a transfer student. The course work completed at the original college is called transfer work. Many colleges have rules regarding the number of credit hours that a student can transfer. Most colleges will not accept credit from another college if the grade in the course is lower than a C.

V

VETERANS' AFFAIRS Many colleges have an Office of Veterans' Affairs to assist those students who have served in the military. Colleges often accept credit earned by a veteran while in the service. Veterans' financial packages are also often different because of the GI Bill.

VICE-PRESIDENT Many colleges have several vice-presidents who serve under the president. These are senior-level administrators who assist with the daily operations of the college and may include vice-presidents of academic affairs, financial affairs, and student affairs, among others.

VOLUMES A *volume* refers to a book or a piece of nonprint material that assists students in their studies. If a college library has 70,000 volumes, it means that the library has 70,000 books and other pieces of media. Many colleges have millions of volumes.

W

WHO'S WHO This is the shortened title of Who's Who in American Colleges and Universities. Students are nominated by the college for this national recognition because of their academic standing and their achievements in co-curricular activities and community service.

WOMEN'S STUDIES Some colleges offer majors and minors in women's studies. The curriculum is centered on the major contributions of women in art, literature, medicine, history, law, architecture, and sciences.

INDEX
(Italicized page numbers indicate quotations.)

Academic freedom
    benefits of, 229-230
    defined, 265
    professors and, 226-227
Accreditation, defined, 265
Acquired immunodeficiency syndrome, defined, 265
Active listening
    versus passive listening, 116-117
    reasons for, 119-120
    strategies for, 126
Adding (a course), defined, 265
Adler, M., *12*
Administration, defined, 265
Advising, defined, 265
Advisors, 251
African-American studies, defined, 265
AIDS, defined, 265
Alumna/alumnus/alumni, defined, 265
America Online, defined, 265
Analytical thinking
    brain function and, 83
    characteristics of, 86-88
    school settings and, 84
AOL (America Online), defined, 265
Apollinaire, Guillaume, *36*
Articulation agreement, defined, 265
Associate degree, defined, 265
Attendance
    defined, 265
    note taking and, 135-136
    studying and, 157-158
Auditing, defined, 265
Auditory learners, 94

Babe Ruth, 41
Baccalaureate degree, defined, 265-266
Board of Trustees, defined, 266
Brain function, in information processing, 83-84, 89
    memory styles and, 95. *See also* Memory
    teaching styles and, 230

Campus, defined, 266
Campus police, defined, 266
Campus resources. *See* Resources
Career center, 251-252
Career counselors, 255
Career planning, 245-262
    career counselors and, 255
    doing versus being, 248-250
    mentors and, 253-254
    personal success plan, 259-260
    publications on, 260
    research in, 256
    self-analysis exercises/studies
        career choices, 247-248
        career decision making, 246
        career research plan, 261-262
    steps to, 250-252
Career research plan, 261-262
Carrel, defined, 266
Casey, John, 41
Catalog (college)
    contents and use of, 206-209
    defined, 266
Certificate program, defined, 266
Churchill, Winston, 35
Class assignments, analysis of, 226-227

Class standing, definitions of
    first-year, 268
    junior, 269
    senior, 271
    sophomore, 271
Classes. *See* Courses
Classroom etiquette, 234-235
CLEP program, defined, 266
Cognate, defined, 266
College catalog
    contents and use of, 206-209
    defined, 266
College Level Examination Program, defined, 266
Communications, course requirements, defined, 266
Comprehensive exams, defined, 266
Computer resources, 210-211
Context clues, 163-164
Continuing education, defined, 266
Coolidge, Calvin, *48*
Co-op experience, defined, 266
Co-requisite, defined, 266
Cornell system, 143-144
Counseling services, 213
    defined, 266
Counselors, career, 255
Course title, defined, 266-267
Courses. *See also individual areas of study*
    adding, defined, 265
    auditing, defined, 265
    dropping, defined, 267
    load, defined, 269
    title, defined, 266-267
Credit hour, defined, 267
Curriculum, defined, 267

Daydreaming. *See* Dreaming
Dean, defined, 267
Dean's list, defined, 267
Degree, defined, 267
Dictionary of Occupational Titles, 256
Diploma, defined, 267
Disney, Walt, 35
DOT. *See Dictionary of Occupational Titles*
Dreaming, career planning and, 247-248, 250-251
Dropping (a course), defined, 267
Drucker, Peter, *60*

Einstein, Albert, 35
Electives
    career planning and, 251
    defined, 267
Emeriti, defined, 267
Emerson, Ralph Waldo, *28, 106, 242*
Essay questions, 197-199
Etiquette, classroom, 234-235
Evening college, defined, 267
Exams, comprehensive, defined, 266
Exercises. *See also* Self-studies
    on career choices, 247-248
    career research plan, 261-262
    class assignments, analysis of, 226-227
    college catalog, awareness and use of, 208
    on fear, 38-40
    on library research, 209-210
    on meeting with professors, 236-237
    on mentors, 254
    on motivation, 50, 52

on potential, 13-14
resource inventory, 218
on self-esteem, 19-22
SQ3R study method, use of, 170-176
on study time allocation, 69, 71-72
teachers versus professors, rating of, 225-226
on teaching others, 90-91
on test anxiety, 189
on textbook features, 167
vocabulary, 163-164
External goals, internal goals versus, motivation and, 50-51

Faculty, defined, 267
Fear
conquering of, 36-38, 40-41
self-analysis exercise, 38-40
test anxiety, controlling, 188-190
Federal family education loans, 214
Federal supplemental educational opportunity grants, 214
Fees, defined, 267
FFEL loans, 214
Financial aid
application strategies, 216-217
defined, 267
eligibility requirements, 214-215
publications on, 215
services, 213-217
Fine arts, defined, 267-268
First-year student, defined, 268
Foreign language, defined, 268
Fraternity, defined, 268
Friends, as resources, 212-213
FSEOG grants, 214

Gandhi, Mahatma K., *180*
Gerow, Josh R., *95*
Global thinking
brain function and, 84
characteristics of, 87-88
school settings and, 84
Glossary, 265-272
Goal setting
goal statements, preparation of, 44-46
self-analysis exercises/studies
attitudes/behaviors, 34-35
barriers to, 46-48
worksheet, 53-55
Goals
attaining, methods for, 52-53
characteristics of, 41-42
defined, 41
fear and, 36-38
importance of, 42-43
internal versus external, motivation and, 50-51
realistic versus unrealistic, 41-42
setting. *See* Goal setting
short-term versus long-term, 42
types of, 43-44
GPA (Grade Point Average), defined, 268
Graduate students
financial aid restrictions, 214
teaching assistant, defined, 268
Graduate teaching assistant, defined, 268
Grants, 214
defined, 268

Hansberry, Lorraine, 35
Health services, 217
Hearing, listening versus, 106-110
High school teachers, versus professors, 225-227
Higher education
academic freedom in. *See* Academic freedom

admissions policies, 225
defined, 268
professors in. *See* Professors
students in. *See* Students
Highlighting, of textbook, 169
Honor code, defined, 268
Honors, defined, 268
Honors college, defined, 268
Humanities, defined, 268

ID (Identification cards), defined, 268-269
Income, career planning and, 257
Independent study, defined, 269
Information processing
analytical versus global, 83-84, 86-88
learning and. *See* Learning
listening and. *See* Listening
self-analysis exercises/studies
attitudes/behaviors, 83
inventory, 84-86
strategies, 97
teaching styles and, 230
Internal versus external goals, motivation and, 50-51
Inventories
of campus resources, 218
on information processing, 84-86
on learning preference, 92-93
personality, 255, 256
Strong-Campbell Interest Inventory, 255

Joubert, Joseph, 222
Journal, defined, 269
Junior, defined, 269

Kinesthetic learners, 94

Learning
learning preference inventory, 92-93
learning preference theory, 89-90
listening and. *See* Listening
memory and, 95
strategies for, 91, 93-94, 97
styles of, 91, 93-94
teaching exercise, 90-91
teaching styles and, 230
via mnemonic devices, 95-96
Learning resource centers, 211
Lecture, defined, 269
Liberal arts, defined, 269
Library, as resource, 209-210
Lincoln, Abraham, 35
Listening, 106-120, 126
active style of
versus passive listening, 116-117
reasons for, 119-120
strategies for, 126
definitions of, 110-112
for key words, phrases, and hints, 118-119
in L-STAR note taking-system, 138
obstacles to, 113-117
Listening skills
listening versus hearing, 106-110
self-analysis exercises/studies, 105, 120-125
Listening strategies, 117-118, 126
Load (class/course), defined, 269
Loans
eligibility requirements, 214-215
publications on, 215
types of, 214
Long-term goals, short-term goals versus, 42
Long-term memory, 95
L-STAR system, 137-141

Macy, R. H., 41
Major, defined, 269
Malcolm X, 36
Mapping system, of note taking, 145-147
Matching questions, 194
Math study techniques, 177-179
Meal plan, defined, 269
Memory
   in L-STAR system of note taking, 141
   mnemonic devices for, 95-96
   types, 95
Mentors
   career planning and, 253-254
   defined, 253, 269
Minor, defined, 269
Mistakes, self-esteem and, 27
Mnemonic devices, 95-96
   ROAR (Receiving, Organizing, Assigning, Reacting), 107-110
Motivation
   goal setting and, 33-35
   importance of, 49-50
   internal versus external goals and, 50-51
   role in achieving success, 14
   self-analysis exercise, 50, 52
Multiple-choice questions, 195-196
Myers-Briggs Personality Type Indicator, 255

Natural sciences, defined, 269
Non-system-imposed time, 63
Note taking, 132-150
   key phrases in, 134-135
   purpose, 133-134
   self-analysis exercises/studies
      attitudes/behaviors, 132-133
      L-STAR method, 139
Note-taking strategies
   Cornell system, 143-144
   general, 135-146, 141-142, 150
   L-STAR system, 137-141
   mapping system, 145-147
   outlining, 142-143

Objectives, goal setting and, 44-46
Organizations, professional, career planning and, 252
Orientation, defined, 269

Passive listening, active listening versus, 116-117
Pell grants, 214
Perkins loans, 214
Personal success plan, 259-260
Personality inventories, 255, 256
Plagiarism, defined, 269
Potential
   discovery and achievement of, 12-14
   self-analysis exercise, 13-14
Powell, 80
Prefix code, defined, 269-270
Preprofessional programs, defined, 270
Prerequisite, defined, 270
President (college), defined, 270
Prioritizing, time management and, 65-66, 75-76
Probation, defined, 270
Procrastination
   in test preparation, 191
   time management and, 74-75
Professional organizations, career planning and, 252
Professor(s)
   academic freedom and, 226-227, 229
   activities and responsibilities of, 227-228
   defined, 270
   expectations of, understanding, 231-232
   high school teachers versus, 225-227
   making an appointment with, 236-237
   professional rankings, 228
   sample schedule, 236
   student attitudes toward. *See* Students
   on students, goals for and opinions of, 232-233
   teaching as career choice, 227
   teaching styles of, 230
Provost, defined, 270
Publications
   on career planning, 260
   on financial aid services, 215
Purkey, W., *17*

Queist, Michael, *64*

Reading, career planning and, 252
Readmit, defined, 270
Realistic versus unrealistic goals, 41-42
Registrar, defined, 270
Research, in career planning, 256
Residence hall, defined, 270
Residency requirement, defined, 270
Resources
   for career planning, 256, 260
   college catalog, 206-209
   counseling services, 213
   Dictionary of Occupational Titles, 256
   financial aid services, 213-216
   friends as, 212-213
   health services, 217
   knowledge of, self-study on, 204-205
   learning resource centers, 211
   library, 209-210
   tangible versus intangible, 205-206
Responsibility, self-esteem and, 24
Risk taking, 25
ROAR (Receiving, Organizing, Assigning, Reacting), 107-110
Robinson, *18*
Rogers, Carl, *154*
Room and board, defined, 270
Roosevelt
   Eleanor, *184*
   Franklin D., *32, 58*

Schedules, professor's, 236
Scholar, defined, 270
Scholarships, 215
Section code, defined, 270-271
Self-esteem
   increasing, methods for, 21, 22-28
   role in achieving success, 14
   self-analysis exercise, 19-22
Self-studies. *See also* Exercises
   on career decision making, 246
   of goal setting, 34-35. *See also* Goal setting
   of information processing, 83
   inventories. *See also* Inventories
      of campus resources, 218
      on information processing, 84-86
      on learning preference, 92-93
   of listening skills, 105
   of note taking, 132-133
   on professors and higher education, 224
   of resource awareness and utilization, 204-205
   of test taking, 187
   of time management, 60-61. *See also* Time management
Self-talk, 25
Senior, defined, 271
Sensory memory, 95
SGA, defined, 271
Shadowing, 252
Shaw, George Bernard, *260-261*

Short-answer questions, 197
Shorthand symbols, 138-139
Short-term goals versus long-term goals, 42
Smith, Sidney, *202*
Social sciences, defined, 271
Sophomore, defined, 271
Sororities, defined, 271
SQ3R study method, 167-169
    practice exercise, 170-176
Staff, defined, 271
Strong-Campbell Interest Inventory, 255
Student Government Association, defined, 271
Student loan, defined, 271
Students
    class standing, definitions of
        first-year, 268
        junior, 269
        senior, 271
        sophomore, 271
    on professors
        attitudes toward and opinions of, 233
        self-study regarding, 224
    professors' expectations of, understanding, 231-232
    professors' opinions on and goals for, 232-233
    transfer, defined, 272
    transient, defined, 271
Study time
    allocation, self-analysis exercise, 69-72
    procrastination and, 74-75
Studying, 157-180
    environment for, 159
    exercises
        SQ3R study method, 170-176
        on textbook features, 167
        vocabulary, 163-164
    math, 177-179
    notes, 176-177. *See also* Note taking
    strategies for, 179
        highlighting of text, 169
        SQ3R method, 167-169
        textbook feature review, 165-167
        vocabulary development, 162-165
    study plan, 72-73, 161
    supplies for, 160-161
    time for. *See* Study time
Success, defined, 11
Supplies, for studying, 160-161
Survey, question, read, recite, review study method. *See* SQ3R study method
Suspension, defined, 271
Syllabus, 231
    defined, 271
System-imposed time, 62

Teachers
    graduate teaching assistant, defined, 268
    versus professors, 225-227
Teaching styles, 230
Tenure, defined, 271
Test of English as a Foreign Language, defined, 271
Tests
    anxiety over, controlling, 188-190
    comprehensive exams, defined, 266
    preparation styles, 190-192
    purpose of, 188
    taking. *See* Test-taking strategies

Test-taking strategies, 187-199
    controlling test anxiety, 188-190
    for essay questions, 197-199
    general, 192-194
    for matching questions, 194
    for multiple-choice questions, 195-196
    self-study of, 187
    for short-answer questions, 197
    for true/false questions, 195
Textbooks
    feature review of, 165-167
    highlighting of, 169
    SQ3R study method, 167-169
Thoreau, Henry David, *248*
Thought processes, in information processing. *See* Information processing
Time
    management of. *See* Time management
    passage of
        activity log, 66-67
        perception of, 64-65
    for study. *See* Study time
    types of, 62-63
Time log, 66-67
    analysis of, 67-68
Time management, 59-78
    procrastination and, 74-75
    self-analysis exercises/studies
        attitudes/behaviors, 60-61
        perception of passage of time, 65
        on prioritization, 65-66
        of system-imposed versus non-system-imposed activities, 64
        time log, analysis of, 67-68
        study time, allocation of, 69-72
        time wasters, 73-74
Time wasters, 73-74
TOEFL, defined, 271
Tolkien, J.R.R., *250*
Training, career planning and, 257
Transcript, defined, 271
Transfer, defined, 272
Transient student, defined, 271
Transitional studies, defined, 271-272
Translation of notes, in L-STAR system, 140
True/false questions, 195
Trustees, Board of, defined, 266

Unrealistic goals, realistic goals versus, 41-42

Values auction, 15-16
Veteran's Affairs, Office of, defined, 272
Vice-president (college), defined, 272
Visual learners, 93-94
Vocabulary development, 162-165
    context clues, 163-164
    word analysis, 164-165
Volumes, defined, 272

Ward, William Arthur, *177*
Washington, Booker T., *8*
Who's Who in American Colleges, defined, 272
Winning, self-esteem and, 27
Women's studies, defined, 272
Word analysis, 164-165
Work study, 214
Working memory, 95